Developing a

Servant's Heart

BY

Charles F. Stanley

Thomas Nelson
Since 1798

NASHVILLE   DALLAS   MEXICO CITY   RIO DE JANEIRO

Published in Nashville, Tennessee, by Thomas Nelson, Inc.

Editing, layout, and design by Gregory C. Benoit Publishing, Old Mystic, CT

ISBN 978-1-4185-2811-9

Printed in the United States of America

09 10 11 WC 10 9 8 7

Contents

A Fresh Perspective on Servanthood

The Bible is far more than a great piece of literature or a book of inspirational and spiritual truths. It is a very practical manual for daily living. In many ways, it is God's "Service Manual" for life. It tells us how to live a godly life, how to maintain loving relationships, and how to fulfill our reason for being on this earth. It clearly tells us how to use our gifts, time, talents, money, and more for God's glory and His purposes.

From cover to cover, the Bible is filled with examples of men and women who had a servant's heart and who demonstrated loving service to others. Virtually all of the great stories in the Bible fall into one of three categories: 1. God's service to mankind; 2. Mankind's service to God; 3. The service of men and women to each other.

Service is *giving*, and giving is the very essence of the gospel. God *gave* His only begotten Son. Jesus *gave* His life on the cross. We *give* our hearts to God. We are called to *give* of ourselves to others. The Bible tells us how to serve others and also what to expect *when* we serve others. It challenges us to serve with great generosity and unconditional love. As you study God's principles for servanthood, I encourage you to go to your Bible for inspiration as well as guidance. Underline phrases. Highlight words or verses. Make notes in the margins to record the specific ways that God speaks to you.

This book can be used by you alone or by several people in a small-group study. At various times, you will be asked to relate to the material in one of these four ways:

1. **What new insights have you gained?** Make notes about the insights

that you have. You may want to record them in your Bible or in a separate journal. As you reflect back over your insights, you are likely to see how God has moved in your life.

2. *Have you ever had a similar experience?* Each of us approaches the Bible from a unique background—our own particular set of relationships and experiences. Our experiences do not make the Bible true— the Word of God is truth regardless of our opinion about it. It is important, however, to share our experiences in order to see how God's truth can be applied to human lives.

3. *How do you feel about the material presented?* Emotional responses do not give validity to the Scriptures, nor should we trust our emotions as a gauge for our faith. In small-group Bible study, however, it is good for participants to express their emotions. The Holy Spirit often communicates with us through this unspoken language.

4. *In what way do you feel challenged to respond or to act?* God's Word may cause you to feel inspired or challenged to change something in your life. Take the challenge seriously and find ways of acting upon it. If God reveals to you a particular need that He wants *you* to address, take that as "marching orders" from God. God is expecting you to *do* something with the challenge that He has just given you.

Start and conclude your Bible study sessions in prayer. Ask God to give you spiritual eyes to see and spiritual ears to hear. As you conclude your study, ask the Lord to seal what you have learned so that you will never forget it. Ask Him to help you grow into the fullness of the stature of Christ Jesus.

Again, I caution you to keep the Bible at the center of your study. A genuine Bible study stays focused on God's Word and promotes a growing faith and a closer walk with the Holy Spirit in *each* person who participates.

2

LESSON 1

Saved to Serve

❧ In this lesson ☙

LEARNING: WHAT IS GOD'S PURPOSE FOR OUR LIVES? WHY DID HE SAVE US?

GROWING: HOW CAN I BECOME MORE LIKE CHRIST?

Complete the following three statements:

1. God saved me because:

2. God's purpose for saving me was:

3. I am most like Jesus when I:

The purpose for my opening this Bible study with a little quiz is to set the proper framework for our discussion of servanthood. The answers that I am seeking are these:

1. God saved me because *He loves me.*

2. God's purpose for saving me was to *bring Him glory.*

3. I am most like Jesus when I *serve others.*

1. God Saved Me Because *He Loves Me*

The sole reason that God sent His Son Jesus to this world was that He loved us. God forgives us, grants us eternal life, and gives us the gift of His Holy Spirit out of His immeasurable love and grace. There is no other reason.

Many people seem to believe that God saves them because of their good works or service. Nothing could be further from the truth. There isn't any type of service that can earn salvation. The apostle Paul made this very clear when he wrote to the Ephesians: "For by grace you have been saved through faith, and that not of yourselves; it is the gift of God, not of works, lest anyone should boast" (Eph. 2:8–9). Even the faith by which we believe is a gift of God that flows from His love!

If God saved a person on the basis of works, we would have to ask ourselves, "How much good service is enough?" Such a question cannot be answered. There is no amount of good service that can equal the shed blood of Jesus Christ. The gospel is that Jesus Christ shed His blood on the cross to purchase salvation for you and for me. He did so voluntarily and willingly in obedience to His heavenly Father. John 3:16 tells us, "For God so *loved* the world that He gave His only begotten Son, that whoever believes in Him should not perish but have everlasting life."

Just as a person is not saved because of his past good works, neither is a person saved because he has potential for future good works. God does not look at one person and say, "You have the potential to be a preacher, so I am going to save you" and then look at another and say, "You aren't worth much, so I won't save you." God's gift of salvation is offered freely to all who will receive it. God created each one of us with a unique set of talents and traits that can be employed for His service as He wills. No person is without merit in His eyes; all are worthy of salvation.

There is also no inherent "goodness" in any person that warrants his salvation. No person has the prerogative to stand before God Almighty and say, "I deserve to be saved." Rather, we each must confess, "I *need* to be saved." Romans 3:23 says, "For all have sinned and fall short of the glory of God."

This point is critical for you to understand at the outset of this study on service: Developing a servant's heart is something that we do in *response* to God's gracious gifts of salvation, eternal life, and the Holy Spirit. It is never something that we do in order to *earn* salvation—to win, warrant, or put ourselves into a position to deserve it.

∽

∽ Have you accepted Christ as your Lord and Savior? If not, what is hindering you?

☙ If so, what is your attitude toward serving others?

2. God's Purpose for Saving Me Was *to Bring Him Glory*

God saved us so that we might be His "trophies"—we might be examples to others of God's love and mercy at work in and through a human life.

Many people think that the reason for salvation is so that they might go to heaven when they die. Eternal life is part of God's forgiveness plan for us, but that is not the sole reason for our salvation. We are saved so that we might be "redeemed"—we once were in slavery to something that was evil, but we have been rescued and set free from sin so that we might live a life of righteousness before God. If God's only purpose for our salvation was so that we might go to heaven, He would be doing each of us a great favor by saving us and then immediately slaying us.

God's purpose for saving us is that we might reflect His nature—we might be His people on earth, doing the kinds of works that Jesus Himself would do if He were walking in our shoes. God desires to manifest His character through our personalities and gifts. When we allow His Holy Spirit to work in and through us, we become vessels of His love in action. We reflect His compassion, love, and mercy to others. And in so doing, we are His witnesses. We bring credit, honor, and glory to *Him*.

God does not save us in order that we might be part of an elite group of "good people." He saves us in order that we might reach out to all people with God's goodness. He does not put us in the church so that we might soak up sermons, Bible conferences, prayer meetings, and seminars. He puts us in the church so that we might be of good use to those who are in need—so that we might function as His body, using our gifts, talents, and skills as the Holy Spirit directs to help one another. This is an important point for you to consider as we begin this Bible study. God did not save you simply so that you can have the assurance that you are going to heaven one day. He saved you in order that you might live every hour of every day of the remainder of your life in faithful service and obedience to Jesus Christ.

What does it mean to be God's "trophy"?

What sort of a trophy has your life been in the past?

❦

3. I Am Most Like Jesus When I *Serve Others*

The foremost characteristic of the life of Jesus Christ is *service*. We are most like Him when we serve as He served.

Many think that a person is most like Jesus when he preaches as Jesus preached, teaches as Jesus taught, heals as Jesus healed, or performs miracles as Jesus performed miracles. They look only at the outward manifestation of a person's witness and ministry. They need to look beyond the outer manifestation to the *motivation* for Jesus' life: service. Jesus preached, taught, healed, and performed miracles in order to help others, never to call attention to Himself. He poured out His very life so that others might be saved, never thinking for a moment to save Himself. Time and again, Jesus said to those whom He had helped, "Don't tell anyone what has happened."

The critical point for us to recognize at the outset of this study is that God has called you to serve others just as Jesus served others. He didn't save you or call you to service so that you might be exalted. He saved you so that you might serve others and bring praise and honor to God's holy name.

The good news is that any person who is saved *can* serve God and bring glory to Him. The nature of the ministry is not what is important; what *is* important is the motivation behind our service. God loved us so that we might love others. That's what the Christian life is all about.

Having a clear understanding about why God saved you and what He expects of you may very well be the most important aspect of this entire study. As you prepare, ask yourself these important questions:

&. In what ways do you presently serve other people?

❧ In what ways do you serve God?

❧ How might God be calling you to serve others tomorrow?

❧ Today and Tomorrow ❧

TODAY: GOD WANTS HIS CHILDREN TO GROW IN SERVICE TO HIM AND TO OTHERS.

TOMORROW: I'LL REMEMBER THAT I WAS SAVED TO SERVE, AND WILL LOOK FOR OPPORTUNITIES TO SERVE OTHERS.

❧ Notes and Prayer Requests: ❧

LESSON 2

Called to be a Servant

❧ In This Lesson ❧

LEARNING: WHAT DOES IT MEAN TO BE "POURED OUT LIKE WATER"?

GROWING: HOW WILL I LEARN TO BECOME A "BONDSERVANT OF JESUS CHRIST"?

Jesus came as a servant, not as a superstar. His three-year ministry was a powerful example of servanthood—from His first miracle of changing water to wine at a wedding feast to His sacrificial death on the cross in which His own blood flowed freely for the salvation of all who would believe in Him and receive God's offer of forgiveness from sins.

Jesus made two great statements about servanthood that were references to His own life and sacrificial death—words that are also related to our role as servants today.

Planted Like Wheat

Jesus spoke candidly with His disciples about His impending death and resurrection. Much of what He said they didn't understand fully at the time, but looking back they understood very clearly. John tells in his Gospel about an incident that happened just before Passover. A group of Greeks had come to Jerusalem to worship at the feast, and they asked for a private audience with Jesus. The news that Jesus had raised Lazarus from the dead had spread quickly and widely. Many had lined the path leading into Jerusalem from the Mount of Olives to shout "Hosanna!" and to declare Jesus as the "King of Israel!" (John 12:12–15).

Jesus was being pressured to make a public, political move to consolidate power and become an earthly ruler in place of both the Romans and an oppressive, legalistic Jewish Temple rulership.

The Greeks said to Philip, "Sir, we wish to see Jesus." Philip told Andrew of their request, and they went together to see Jesus. From a human perspective, this could have become a top-level meeting, leading to a human-engineered political coup. Jesus gave this answer: "The hour has come that the Son of Man should be glorified" (John 12:23). On the surface, this statement must have been taken by the disciples to be a strong signal—"Now is the time!" To be glorified means to reach your crowning moment, your shining hour. But then Jesus quickly went on to say this:

> Most assuredly, I say to you, unless a grain of wheat falls into the ground and dies, it remains alone; but if it dies, it produces much grain. He who loves his life will lose it, and he who hates his life in this world will keep it for eternal life.

> —John 12:24–25

Jesus made it very clear that He was not called to be a political king so that people might experience a better earthly existence; rather, He was destined to die a sacrificial death so that man might have eternal life. Jesus' higher and more meaningful goal was not to be achieved by man-made systems and alliances of this world, but rather through the ultimate act of ministry and servanthood—a sacrificial death.

Jesus followed His statement to Philip and Andrew by saying, "If any-one serves Me, let him follow Me; and where I am, there My servant will be also. If anyone serves Me, him My Father will honor" (John 12:26).

Jesus chose the servant role for Himself—which was actually the heav-enly Father's role for Him. He then called His followers to become like Him and to be, first and foremost, *servants*. Jesus concluded, "What shall I say? 'Father, save Me from this hour'? But for this purpose I came to this hour. Father, glorify Your name" (John 12:27). Jesus did not back away from servanthood or the ultimate act of service—His sacrificial death. He did not regard His crucifixion in any way to be a demeaning or diminishing act, but He considered it to be the very pur-pose for His life and the fulfillment of His time on this earth. His entire life and ministry had been aimed at this supreme act of service.

"Make sure that what you are living for is what you are willing to die for." That's the way that Jesus lived. He lived a life of service, and He died a death that was an act of service.

🙠 What new insights do you have into the way Jesus was a servant?

🙠 List one or two people who have served you in a Christ-like way. What did they do that was meaningful? How did they affect your life?

Poured out Like Water

Psalm 22 is a prophetic psalm linked very closely to the crucifixion of Jesus. It contains this phrase: "I am poured out like water" (v. 14).

The very life essence of Jesus was poured out like water. During His life, He poured Himself out on all those who were hungry and thirsty for the things of God. He gave of Himself freely to all who came to Him in need. He said to a woman by a well in Samaria, "Whoever drinks of the water that I shall give him will never thirst. But the water that I shall give him will become in him a fountain of water springing up into everlasting life" (John 4:14). In His crucifixion, blood and water mingled freely, flowing from Jesus' side. He willingly gave His life, His blood "poured out" for the sins of the world.

The purpose of being "planted" like a grain of wheat or "poured out" like water is not the sacrificial giving itself, but rather what follows such service: a great blessing and reward. When a grain of wheat is planted, the seed dies, but it brings an abundant harvest. The single dying grain produces "much grain" (John 12:24). In pouring Himself out, Jesus intended that His own spirit become a "fountain of water springing up" (John 4:14).

Death or sacrifice in itself is not the goal. Being a servant is not having a martyr's complex—a desire to die just for the sake of dying. Rather, our life is to be poured out in loving service so that what we give bears the quality of life in it. In pouring ourselves out to others, others can experience greater life, and we experience a more purposeful life. The end result is not a moot death but a glorious everlasting abundance.

It was because servanthood brings about a great blessing that Jesus called His disciples, including you and me, to be servants.

Among the many benefits of servanthood are these:

&. A radiant excitement in your life for God and for all things that are good

&. A healing in your life

&. A difference in the lives of those whom you serve

&. Inspiration and motivation to those who benefit from and who witness your generous service

&. A more fruitful life, both in the natural and supernatural realms

Most assuredly, I say to you, unless a grain of wheat falls into the ground and dies, it remains alone; but if it dies, it produces much grain. He who loves his life will lose it, and he who hates his life in this world will keep it for eternal life. If anyone serves Me, let him follow Me; and where I am, there My servant will be also. If anyone serves Me, him My Father will honor.

—John 12:24-26

&. What do Jesus' words above teach you about the cost of being a servant?

≈ What do you learn about the rewards of service?

≈≈≈

Like Master, Like Servant

The disciples of Jesus had a very clear understanding of their role as servants. Note how the disciples described themselves:

≈ "Simon Peter, a bondservant and apostle of Jesus Christ" (2 Peter 1:1)

≈ "James, a bondservant of God and of the Lord Jesus Christ" (James 1:1)

≈ "Paul and Timothy, bondservants of Jesus Christ" (Phil. 1:1)

≈ "Paul, a bondservant of Jesus Christ, called to be an apostle" (Rom. 1:1)

The Greek word that is generally translated as "bondservant" in the New Testament is a word that was also used to refer to the "lower rowers"—the galley slaves who were kept in chains below the decks of large ships. They did the exhausting, difficult, and unseen work of rowing vessels across the seas and through the storms. There is nothing about this image that brings about the praise and admiration of others, since the work goes mostly unrecognized and unrewarded by mankind.

15

Yet this is the word that the disciples used to describe themselves in their work on behalf of others; they saw it as an honor to be a bondservant of Christ Jesus, a "lower rower" in the work of God's kingdom.

This concept of success is completely inverted from that of the world's standard. The world tells us that the successful person is the one at the top, the one who is most visible, most accomplished. The Scriptures tell us that in God's eyes, the successful person is the one who is willing to be a lower rower for the benefit of others and for the sake of the gospel.

∂. How do you imagine it would feel to be a "lower rower" on a ship in the first century? How does it feel at times to be a "lower rower" in the kingdom of God?

∂. List a few things that you would consider "lower rower" positions of service. Why are they so unattractive to you?

༄

The disciples recognized the blessing that came from being a bondservant. They knew that their efforts in the spiritual realm were cause for
joy because they were helping others to find eternal life in Christ Jesus.
Paul wrote to the Philippians from a jail cell, "If I am being poured out
as a drink offering on the sacrifice and service of your faith, I am glad
and rejoice with you all" (Phil. 2:17).

The disciples fully embraced their role as servants. They knew this to be
their calling and identity, *not because they were leaders of the church*,
but because they were following in the steps of Jesus Christ, the first
and foremost Servant of God. We are called to be servants today, and
to have the heart of a servant as our hallmark, regardless of the area in
which we serve the church or the role that we fill. Servanthood is to be
our attitude and our motivation as we follow Christ Jesus our Lord.

Some people feel that it is only pastors or other members of a church
staff who are God's servants. In reality, any person who has accepted
Jesus Christ as Savior is called to be a servant of God and to be God's
minister to others in particular areas of need, at particular times, but
always with a mind and a heart motivated toward generous service.

Nobody is excluded from service. We each are called to serve God and
to serve others in need every day of our lives. Ephesians 2:10 tells us:

> For we are His workmanship, created in Christ Jesus for good
> works, which God prepared beforehand that we should walk
> in them.

Service is the *doing* of good works *as God leads and directs* through
the power of the Holy Spirit. The works are there for us to do. Our
responsibility is to obey God, even as Jesus obeyed the Father, and to

17

serve Him with *all* of our lives—every last grain, every last bit "poured out" to Him and to others.

❧ What does it mean to be God's "workmanship"?

❧ How do you reconcile the fact that you were "created in Christ Jesus for good works" with the fact that your salvation is by faith alone, not involving any good works on your part?

❧ How is the Lord challenging you to reevaluate your concept of service? In what ways is the Lord challenging you to engage in more active servanthood?

Let this mind be in you, which was also in Christ Jesus: Who, being in the form of God, thought it not robbery to be equal with God: But made himself of no reputation, and took upon him the form of a servant, and was made in the likeness of men.

—Philippians 2:5-7

What does it mean that Christ "made Himself of no reputation"?

What does it mean to "let this mind be in you, which was also in Christ Jesus"? What was Jesus' "mindset"? How does *your* mindset compare?

❧ Today and Tomorrow ❧

TODAY: JESUS AND HIS DISCIPLES SET THE EXAMPLE FOR ME OF BECOMING
A BONDSERVANT OF CHRIST.

TOMORROW: I WILL NOT RUN AWAY FROM OPPORTUNITIES TO SERVE, EVEN
IF IT MEANS BEING A "LOWER ROWER."

❧ Notes and Prayer Requests: ❧

Lesson 3

A Servant's Spirit

❧ In This Lesson ❧

LEARNING: WHAT ARE THE THREE MARKS OF A TRUE SERVANT?

GROWING: HOW CAN WE LEARN TO SERVE WITHOUT EXPECTING ANY RE-
WARD?

The world has a hierarchy, a "ladder," for evaluating the success of a person. Sometimes that ladder is based upon fame, sometimes upon money. The person who has made his way to the position of CEO is considered to be at the top of the ladder.

This is not new to our century or to modern man. Jesus had to deal with this thinking among His own disciples. In fact, even during the Last Supper, a dispute arose among the disciples "as to which of them should be considered the greatest" (Luke 22:24). It wasn't the first time that this had happened. Several times in the course of Jesus' ministry we find a concern expressed about position and authority. Read Luke 22:25–27, where Jesus speaks to His disciples at the Last Supper.

This concept seemed completely upside down to the disciples, that service should equal greatness. It was a perspective that went against the grain, against common sense, against the prevailing world opinion. And it still does. If a person engages in servanthood all the time, he is considered to be a wimp, a chump, a doormat. The person who is widely admired by the masses tends to be the person who has shown himself to have the most power, the most appeal, the most intelligence, the most money, and the most accomplishment—the one at the top of the scale.

God does not deal in hierarchies. He deals only in categories. A person is either saved or unsaved. A person is either following God in obedience or rebelling against God. A person is either a servant or not a servant.

When have you been treated like a "doormat"? Why were you treated that way? How did you respond?

What are your greatest goals and aspirations in life? If you could only accomplish one thing before you die, what would it be?

A Simple Definition

Jesus gave a very simple definition of service in John 12:25 when He said:

He who loves his life will lose it, and he who hates his life in this world will keep it for eternal life.

The person who loves his life is the person who is self-centered, selfish, greedy—the one who lives totally for his own benefit. This is the person who desires to be *served*. In the end, he will lose everything that he has ever attempted to gain for himself. The person who "hates" his life is the person who is willing to put others first—the one who gives and helps others. This is the person who is a *servant*. In the end, Jesus said, this is the person who will enter into eternal life.

Some people confuse "hating one's life" with having low self-esteem or with diminishing one's gifts. We are to value ourselves highly. We are to recognize that we are wonderful, unique creations of God. Each of us has been given a set of gifts, traits, and talents by God. We have been designed with a specific purpose in mind—we *are* God's workmanship (Eph. 2:10). We are God's treasure, His delight, His chosen vessels, His beloved children. The fact is, God valued us so highly that He sent His Son, Jesus Christ, to die on the cross so that we might be reconciled to God and live with Him forever. God's love alone gives our lives great value!

In recognizing our great value to God, we have a servant's spirit when we are willing to *use* our gifts for the benefit of others and not solely to bring applause, recognition, or reward to ourselves. We "hate ourselves," from God's standpoint, when we completely abandon our own self-advancement in order to help others in need or to fulfill whatever call of the gospel God has placed upon our lives.

What happens in a very practical way is that those who love their lives tend to hate the lives of other people. They use, abuse, and manipulate others for their own purposes. Those who "hate" their lives are those who choose to love others more than they love their own advancement. They bless, give to, and benefit others.

This is the quality of life that Jesus lived. He didn't dislike Himself or hate the call of God on His life. He knew who He was, and He fully embraced what His heavenly Father had commanded Him to be and to do. But He didn't exalt Himself, seek His own fame and power, or attract attention to Himself. His purpose was to bring glory to the Father and to obey the Father in all things. His purpose was to serve.

Jesus taught, "To whom much is given, from him much will be required" (Luke 12:48). The more we recognize all that we have been given by God—including God's greatest gift to us, our salvation—the more we should recognize that we are required to give much in the way of service. Those who have the greater talents are required to give the greater service.

Paul wrote to the Philippians that Jesus emptied Himself of His heavenly possessions and identity when He became a bondservant of God and took on the likeness of mankind. He "made Himself of no reputation" (Phil. 2:7). That does not mean that Jesus wasn't worthy or deserving of a good reputation—He had the ultimate reputation in that He never sinned against God or man—but that He didn't concern Himself with the world's opinion of Him. As one person said, "Jesus gave Himself to death." Some people work themselves to death in order to get ahead in life, but it is the person who follows Jesus' example and gives himself to death who receives the great rewards in eternity.

✎. What does it mean that Jesus "gave Himself to death"? How might you imitate that attitude this week?

⮞ What things has God given you that He wants you to share with others? Consider time, money, talents, and so forth.

⌘

Three Marks of Servanthood

The person with a genuine servant's heart is a person who bears these attributes:

I. A True Servant does not Demand Recognition

A servant is willing to remain in the shadows or the "lower galleys." The servant gives without acknowledgment; in fact, he is willing to give so that nobody knows who has done the giving. Jesus had strong words about those who try hard to receive the praise of other people. He taught:

Take heed that you do not do your charitable deeds before men, to be seen by them. Otherwise you have no reward from your Father in heaven. Therefore, when you do a charitable deed, do not sound a trumpet before you as the hypocrites do in the synagogues and in the streets, that they may have glory from men. Assuredly, I say to you, they have their reward.

—Matt. 6:1–2

The reward received by those who seek praise from people is just that and only that—praise from people. Such praise comes and goes very quickly; the approval of people is very fickle and often fleeting. God's praise and blessing, on the other hand, are reserved for those who serve others without any expectation of recognition or praise from people.

I am continually amazed at how many people in the body of Christ only want to participate in various aspects of their churches if their names are listed on the committee roster, published in the service bulletin, or engraved on a plaque at the church entrance. I was told recently by the development officer for an organization that fewer and fewer projects are named in "honor" of major contributors; the prevailing practice, rather, is to include the naming of a building, hospital wing, or park as a part of the negotiating process for securing the donation in the first place. As Jesus said, those who desire public acclaim have their reward—but it is not an eternal reward granted by God.

⌘. How do you feel when you don't receive recognition for something that you have done?

⌘. When have you performed some "selfless act" that was secretly motivated by a desire for recognition?

2. A True Servant does not Demand Reward

A servant gives without expecting anything in return from the person that he has served. True servanthood is void of manipulation or a desire to control others.

The best thing that could happen to a slave or a servant in the ancient world was to have a kind, benevolent master. A servant in such a household knew that all of his needs would be met to the greatest degree possible; such a servant had a sense of security and safety. He was not merely the property of the master or "lord," but was considered a valuable asset to be nurtured and rewarded.

Abraham apparently was such a master. We read in Genesis 24:2 that Abraham's oldest servant "ruled over all that he had," and Abraham entrusted him to travel a great distance by himself to find a wife for Isaac, Abraham's son. This servant was faithful to his duty. He had no thought of escaping to "freedom" with Abraham's ten camels and the considerable wealth entrusted to him.

Joseph was a favored servant in the household of the Egyptian Potiphar, who "left all that he had in Joseph's hand" (Gen. 39:6).

Our role as a bondservant of Christ Jesus is of a similar nature. Jesus Christ is our *Lord*. He is our Master, our Ruler, our Owner. He is the One who has redeemed our lives from death. He is the One from whom we take our daily orders and from whom we receive all that we need. He is the One who has entrusted us to conduct spiritual business in His name.

A genuine servant knows that he has all that he needs in Christ Jesus, all that is truly important, all that is desirable and of value. When we give, we *will* receive. But what comes back to us will be from God's

27

hand and at God's command. We are to expect to receive from God *not* because we have given, but because God is faithful in providing for His children, often through supernatural means.

Expecting God to provide for us out of His great storehouse of blessing is far different from *demanding* that God provide for us or reward us because of what we have done. Expecting from God is a mark of faith. Demanding God to act on our behalf is a mark of pride.

> And do not seek what you should eat or what you should drink, nor have an anxious mind. For all these things the nations of the world seek after, and your Father knows that you need these things.
>
> —Luke 12:29-30

⁊ What does it mean to have "an anxious mind"? How does an anxious mind affect your service to others and to the Lord?

⁊ If we truly do not worry about what we'll eat for our next meal, how might that affect our service to others? How can we gain that attitude?

28

3. A True Servant does not Demand Self-Rights

A servant has a "yielded" spirit, both to God and to others. A servant will stand up for what is right in God's eyes, but a person with a genuine servant's heart does not insist that he have his own way. A servant "yields the right of way" to others, or as Paul wrote, "giving preference to one another" (Rom. 12:10).

The hallmark of the Christian life is reflected in Ephesians 5:20–21:

> Giving thanks always for all things to God the Father in the name of our Lord Jesus Christ, submitting to one another in the fear of God.

We are to love God with all of our heart, soul, and mind, and our neighbors as ourselves. It is out of love that we serve. In fact, service is the manifestation of love. If you love, but you do not give to a person and are not generous in your service to that person, on what grounds can you truly say that you love? Service is the evidence of genuine love. It is love in action.

> Jesus said to him, "'YOU SHALL LOVE THE LORD YOUR GOD WITH ALL YOUR HEART, WITH ALL YOUR SOUL, AND WITH ALL YOUR MIND.' This is the first and great commandment. And the second is like it: 'YOU SHALL LOVE YOUR NEIGHBOR AS YOURSELF.'"

> —Matthew 22:37-39

 Notice that Jesus does *not* say, "you shall learn to love yourself in order to love others." What does this suggest about our culture's emphasis on self-esteem and self-love?

29

 In what way is the second command ("love your neighbor") like the first command ("love the Lord your God")? How are the two commands dependent upon one another?

A Serious Challenge

If most of us were asked, "Are you God's servant?" we would probably respond, "Yes, I am. He is my King; I am His subject." The more difficult questions to answer, however, are these: "Do you truly have a servant's heart? Are you willing to serve, and are you presently serving others without demanding recognition, rewards, or 'rights'?"

Many people only give lip service to servanthood. They say that they are servants, want to be servants, or wish that they were better servants. The truth is, we can all grow in our desire, ability, and effectiveness as servants. We must, however, actually *be* servants—not just talk about being servants. James said:

> Be doers of the word, and not hearers only, deceiving yourselves. For if anyone is a hearer of the word and not a doer, he is like a man observing his natural face in a mirror; for he observes himself, goes away, and immediately forgets what kind of man he was. But he who looks into the perfect law of liberty and continues in it, and is not a forgetful hearer but a doer of the work, this one will be blessed in what he does.
>
> —James 1:22–25

The true servant is one who has a heart for service, one who is actually engaged in serving.

> For this is the will of God, that by doing good you may put to silence the ignorance of foolish men—as free, yet not using liberty as a cloak for vice, but as bondservants of God.

> —1 Peter 2:15-16

❧ What does it mean to use liberty "as a cloak for vice"? Give examples of how this is done in the church today. Give examples of how you have done this yourself in the past.

❧ What does it mean to "put to silence the ignorance of foolish men"? How can doing good accomplish this?

But when you do a charitable deed, do not let your left hand know what your right hand is doing, that your charitable deed may be in secret; and your Father who sees in secret will Himself reward you openly.

—Matthew 6:3-4

What does it mean to "not let your left hand know what your right hand is doing"? Why is this principle important in serving God?

When have you seen God rewarding you openly for "charitable deeds" which you have done "in secret"?

And if you do good to those who do good to you, what credit is that to you? For even sinners do the same. And if you lend to those from whom you hope to receive back, what credit is that to you? For even sinners lend to sinners to receive as much back. But love your enemies, do good, and lend, hoping for nothing in return; and your reward will be great, and you will be sons of the Most High. For He is kind to the unthankful and evil.

—Luke 6:33-35

How do we balance the command to love our enemies with the need to stand firm against evil? Where does service to others fit into this balance?

Why does Jesus command us to "lend" to others, rather than commanding us to *give* to others? How does this add insight to the question above?

Today and Tomorrow

TODAY: THE THREE MARKS OF A TRUE SERVANT ARE NOT DEMANDING RECOGNITION, REWARD, OR RIGHTS.

TOMORROW: I WILL PRAYERFULLY WORK ON SERVING OTHERS WITHOUT DEMANDING ANYTHING IN RETURN.

LESSON 4

Jesus: Our Role Model as Servant

☙ In This Lesson ❧ ─────

LEARNING: WHAT SORTS OF PEOPLE DID JESUS SERVE?

GROWING: WHAT SHOULD BE *MY* ATTITUDE WHEN SERVING UNPLEASANT PEOPLE?

─────

One of the names given to Jesus in the New Testament is "Son of David." For many people, this title evokes the kingship of Jesus—and rightfully so. David was a great king, and Jesus is our King of kings.

In Acts 13:36, however, we read this perspective on the life of King David from the apostle Paul: "For David, after he had served his own generation by the will of God." David was not regarded by the first disciples of Jesus primarily as a great soldier, statesman, king, or psalmist, but as a *servant.* David was perceived as being used by God for God's purposes. He functioned as a servant of God to the people of Israel. Servanthood under God's command and authority was David's most important trait.

In this way, Jesus is most assuredly like David. He was and is the supreme Servant. Both David and Jesus knew the secret for true success from God's perspective: *Discover God's goals for your life and then achieve those goals.* God's goals for David were that he unify God's people into one nation, create a centralized place for worship, place a

34

renewed emphasis upon praise before God, and defeat the enemies of God. In fulfilling these goals, David *served*.

God's goal in sending Jesus to this earth was that Jesus might show us what God is like, through both word and deed, revealing to us a loving, healing, saving, and delivering heavenly Father. God's goal was also that Jesus might become the definitive and universal sacrifice for the sins of all mankind. In fulfilling these goals, Jesus *served*.

⁓ What goals do you believe God has for you? How is fulfilling those goals your means of serving God?

A Life of Service

We often think of Jesus' ministry, or His years of "active service," as being the final three years of His life on earth. What we often fail to recognize is that, for nearly 30 years, Jesus *served* His family. The historical tradition within the Christian church is that Joseph, Jesus' earthly father, died when Jesus was a young man, perhaps even a young teenager. As the eldest son in the family, Jesus became responsible for the general well-being of His mother and His earthly brothers and sisters. In all likelihood, Jesus filled this role in a very practical way: providing the family income and helping in the training of his younger siblings.

It was in serving His family that Jesus no doubt developed a great deal of the compassion that we see in Him during His ministry years: He reached out to children, He touched lepers, He embraced outcasts. Compassion is a trait that is part of Jesus' *humanity* as much as His divinity. One does not develop overnight this ability to care for others; it was a pattern that had grown in Jesus throughout His years of caring for His own family.

🕭 How do you feel about the service that you give your family? How do you feel it compares with the way that Jesus cared for His family?

A Profound Act of Service

One of the most profound acts of service in Jesus' life occurred during the Last Supper that He shared with His disciples before the Crucifixion. As you read through these verses, mark those words and phrases that stand out in a special way to you.

[Jesus] rose from supper and laid aside His garments, took a towel and girded Himself. After that, He poured water into a basin and began to wash the disciples' feet, and to wipe them with the towel with which He was girded ... He said to them, "Do you know what I have done to you? You call Me Teacher and Lord, and you say well, for so I am. If I then, your Lord and Teacher, have washed your feet, you also ought to wash one another's feet. For I have given you an example, that you should do as I have done to you. Most assuredly, I say to you, a servant is not greater than his master; nor is he who is sent greater than he who sent him. If you know these things, blessed are you if you do them."

—John 13:4, 5, 12–17

🐦 Why did Jesus wash the disciples' feet?

🐦 In this passage, Peter expresses shock that Jesus would do such a thing. Why? What does that teach us about the types of service that Christ's followers should be willing to perform?

What Jesus was most concerned about in washing the feet of His disciples was that they see His attitude and character of ministry. Jesus used a vivid means of demonstration so that His disciples would never forget His principal truth to them: You must be the servants of one another.

We know from another of the Gospel accounts (Luke 22:24) that the disciples were disputing at the Last Supper which of them was to be considered the greatest. Jesus' response to this dispute was to perform an act of service.

Normally, the host of a home would provide servants to wash the feet of guests as they entered the house from the dusty streets. Guests were expected to come to banquets having bathed and wearing clean garments. This is what Jesus meant, in part, when He said, "You are already bathed; now you are fully clean" (v. 10). His meaning went deeper, however. Jesus was referring to their spiritual nature. He explained,

"You are already clean because of the word which I have spoken to you. Abide in Me, and I in you" (John 15:3–4). He knew that all but one of the disciples, Judas, had fully believed the words of Jesus and were abiding in Him. Judas, however, had chosen to harbor rebellion in his heart and was *not* abiding fully in the words of Jesus.

Why did Peter initially balk at having Jesus wash his feet? One of the reasons may have been that Peter was sitting at the "foot" of the table. In occupying that position during the supper, it was his responsibility to be the servant of the table. If feet needed washing, it should have been Peter who was doing the foot washing. Peter may have felt embarrassed that Jesus was preparing to do what he should have done.

Jesus insisted on washing Peter's feet, however, against Peter's protests. He wanted Peter to see very clearly that unless he learned to receive from Jesus all that He desired to do for him, Peter would not be in a position to serve others. It is only as we receive service from Jesus that we can become true servants to others.

The lesson to Peter and the other disciples was this: As Jesus served them, so they were to serve others. They were to be just as sensitive as Jesus to the needs of others and just as generous as Jesus in their loving care of others.

The same is true for us. We are to serve others in humility and kindness, just as Jesus washed the dusty feet of His disciples only hours before His arrest and crucifixion.

> Most assuredly, I say to you, a servant is not greater than his master; nor is he who is sent greater than he who sent him. If you know these things, blessed are you if you do them.
>
> —John 13:16-17

∞ According to Jesus' words above, what are we really saying if we consider ourselves to be above certain types of service?

∞ What types of blessings might God bestow upon those who have a true servant's heart?

␜⛒┐

Service to the Least Deserving

It is also important to notice that Jesus washed the feet of Judas. He knelt before the man who would betray Him within a matter of hours in the Garden of Gethsemane. Jesus *knew* what He was doing even as He washed the feet of Judas. He said, "I know whom I have chosen" (John 13:18).

Many people find it easy to serve those who are good people. It is much more difficult to serve those whom we consider to be "bad." It is much harder to take a basin and towel and to kneel before a mean-spirited, deliberately rebellious, or hardened person. Jesus, however, is our example. He washed the feet of the man who was the ultimate hypocrite—pleasant to His face but opposed to Him in his heart.

☙ When have you been required to serve someone who was unlovable or difficult to please? How did you feel about your service?

☙ When have you been served by someone, even though you knew that you were not being Christ-like yourself? How did you feel about that person's service to you?

Paul had specific words to say to those who found it difficult to serve their masters. Some members of the first-century church were slaves—some to Christian masters and some to unbelievers. These slaves, free in their spirits in Christ Jesus, nonetheless were called to continue to be servants. These believers were richly blessed and endowed with spiritual gifts, yet they were required to continue to do the most demeaning and humbling acts of service. Consider how the Scripture below applies to *your* service of others.

> Servants, be submissive to your masters with all fear, not only to the good and gentle, but also to the harsh. For this is commendable, if because of conscience toward God one endures grief, suffering wrongfully. For what credit is it if, when you are beaten for your faults, you take it patiently? But when you do good and suffer, if you take it patiently, this is commend-

able before God. For to this you were called, because Christ also suffered for us, leaving us an example, that you should follow His steps:

—1 Peter 2:18-21

🖎 Who might fill the role of "master" in your own life? Your boss? Teacher? The President? Parents? Other?

🖎 How do these verses apply to you in that relationship?

⌒∞⌐

The Most Menial of Tasks

In washing the feet of His disciples, Jesus was engaging in one of the most menial tasks that a household servant performed in the first century. Jesus was sending a clear message that He was willing to do *anything* for His disciples.

Are you willing to do *anything* that God asks of you today? God will never ask you to do anything that is sinful or foolish—neither would bring glory to His name. But God may ask you to do something that is extremely menial.

I have never had a person come to me and say, "Pastor, give me the most menial job in the church. Give me the chore that is the worst to do or the job that is least likely to be recognized." If such a person had come to me, I certainly would have felt that I was in the presence of genuine greatness.

If you are too good for a task, the reality is that you probably are not good enough for it in God's eyes. Any job done "as unto the Lord" is a worthy one, regardless of the nature of the job or the degree of recognition. Is there anybody whose feet you would refuse to wash? That may very well be the person whom God most wants you to serve!

But he who is greatest among you shall be your servant.

—Matthew 23:11

How does this "hierarchy of greatness" compare with what you find in the world—at work, school, in politics, etc.?

How much does your life reflect this attitude?

Serving "As Unto the Lord"

The disciples learned the lesson that Jesus sought to teach them. From the time of Jesus' resurrection onward, they equated all forms of service to others as means of serving Jesus. Jesus had taught them this lesson about service by washing their feet—and also by receiving a special gift from Mary of Bethany. We read in the Gospel of John:

> Six days before the Passover, Jesus came to Bethany, where Lazarus was who had been dead, whom He had raised from the dead. There they made Him a supper; and Martha served, but Lazarus was one of those who sat at the table with Him. Then Mary took a pound of very costly oil of spikenard, anointed the feet of Jesus, and wiped His feet with her hair. And the house was filled with the fragrance of the oil ... Jesus said, ... "She has kept this for the day of My burial."

> —John 12:1–3, 7

Jesus knew how to serve His disciples by washing their feet, but He also knew how to *receive* the service of those who loved and followed Him. He allowed Mary to anoint His feet and to demonstrate her love in this way.

When we serve others, we ultimately are serving Jesus. We are demonstrating our love for Him in the way that we minister to others. Our services to others are also a sign of Jesus' resurrection power and His desire to save and heal all mankind. Our service is the greatest witness that we can give to the Lord Jesus. An act of service is *anything* we do that promotes the kingdom of God, especially those things that are

43

clearly characterized as being righteous, peaceful, and joyous (Rom. 14:17–18).

> For the kingdom of God is not eating and drinking, but righteousness and peace and joy in the Holy Spirit. For he who serves Christ in these things is acceptable to God and approved by men.
>
> —Romans 14:17-18

How are "peace and joy" acts of service to God and to others?

What does this principle teach us about our attitude toward service in general?

The Greatest Service of All

The ultimate service of Jesus can be summed up in one word: Cross. As I indicated at the outset of this lesson, God's goal for Jesus was that He become the sacrifice for our sin. Jesus fulfilled that goal in His death on the cross.

God doesn't let any person get away with sin. Sin causes us to be estranged from God, and God's purpose is always to reach out to us and bring us to reconciliation with Himself. He continues to convict us of our sin until we come to a point of confession. If we fall into sin and error, the Holy Spirit convicts us until we confess, and by His power, repent and live in righteousness before Him.

The soul that sins willfully and continually ultimately dies (Acts 3:23). Jesus was God's supreme means of atonement—of bringing God and man into relationship so that man might be free of guilt and eternal death. It is for this purpose of atonement that Jesus came into this world.

A significant part of God's purpose for your life is that you be a witness to God's love through all that you do and say. You are to be a witness to God's saving power. You are not required by God to die on the cross, but you are called by God to live and die in such a way that others are made increasingly aware of God's plan of forgiveness.

Service cannot be separated from witness or ministry. When you serve others with joy, peace, and righteousness radiating from you, you are a witness to God's love and desire to forgive, a witness to Christ's crucifixion and resurrection, and a witness to the Holy Spirit's empowering and guiding presence. When you serve others, you *are* a minister—you are embodying the work of the Holy Spirit to others.

Without a servant's heart, you may give a *form* of witness or ministry, but you will not be a genuine witness, and your ministry will not bear much fruit. We must have a servant's heart and be motivated by our love for Christ Jesus.

...He said to them, "Whoever desires to come after Me, let him deny himself, and take up his cross, and follow Me.

—Mark 8:34

❧ What does it mean to deny ourselves? How do we do this in everyday life?

❧ What does it mean to take up our cross? How do we do this in everyday life?

Let as many bondservants as are under the yoke count their own masters worthy of all honor, so that the name of God and His doctrine may not be blasphemed. And those who have believing masters, let them not despise them because they are brethren, but rather serve them because those who are benefited are believers and beloved. Teach and exhort these things.

—1 Timothy 6:1-2

❧ What does it mean to count one's master (in this case, meaning boss or other authority figure) as "worthy of all honor"?

How might the "name of God and His doctrine" be blasphemed if we do not show honor to authority figures?

Then Jesus called a little child to Him, set him in the midst of them, and said, "Assuredly, I say to you, unless you are converted and become as little children, you will by no means enter the kingdom of heaven. Therefore whoever humbles himself as this little child is the greatest in the kingdom of heaven.

—Matthew 18:2-4

What does it mean to "become as little children"?

Why does Jesus say that we cannot enter the kingdom of heaven unless we become like children?

Bondservants, obey in all things your masters according to the flesh, not with eyeservice, as men-pleasers, but in sincerity of heart, fearing God. And whatever you do, do it heartily, as to the Lord and not to men, knowing that from the Lord you will receive the reward of the inheritance; for you serve the Lord Christ.

—Colossians 3:22-24

∽. What sort of service is "eyeservice"? How does it differ from genuine service to Christ and others?

∽. How does our service differ if we do it "as to the Lord" rather than "to men"?

∽ Today and Tomorrow ∾

TODAY: JESUS SPENT HIS LIFE SERVING EVERYONE THAT HE MET, NO MATTER HOW UNPLEASANT.

TOMORROW: I WILL PRAYERFULLY STRIVE TO SERVE EVERYONE THAT I MEET—EVEN THOSE WHOM I DON'T LIKE.

Lesson 5

The Pattern for Service

---- 🕊 **In This Lesson** 🕊 ----

Learning: What are the steps of service in practical, day-to-day terms?

Growing: How can I make service to others and God the central habit of my life?

〰️

Service nearly always follows a very specific sequence embodied in the life and ministry of Jesus Christ. A prime example of this sequence is in the way that Jesus dealt with Zacchaeus, a tax collector in Jericho.

Jesus was on His way to Jerusalem for the last time when He met Zacchaeus. He was probably less than two weeks away from His death on the cross. Luke 19:1–10 gives us the story that is the theme for this lesson:

> Then Jesus entered and passed through Jericho. Now behold, there was a man named Zacchaeus who was a chief tax collector, and he was rich. And he sought to see who Jesus was, but could not because of the crowd, for he was of short stature. So he ran ahead and climbed up into a sycamore tree to see Him, for He was going to pass that way. And when Jesus came to the place, He looked up and saw him, and said to him, "Zacchaeus, make haste and come down, for today I must stay at

your house." So he made haste and came down, and received Him joyfully. But when they saw it, they all complained, saying, "He has gone to be a guest with a man who is a sinner."

Then Zacchaeus stood and said to the Lord, "Look, Lord, I give half of my goods to the poor; and if I have taken anything from anyone by false accusation, I restore fourfold."

And Jesus said to him, "Today salvation has come to this house, because he also is a son of Abraham; for the Son of Man has come to seek and to save that which was lost."

The sequence of service is fivefold: awareness, availability, acceptance, abiding, and abandonment. Read through the story about Jesus and Zacchaeus again and circle words and phrases that seem to relate to these terms.

Step 1: Awareness

Zacchaeus was a wealthy, hopeful, desperate man. Luke tells us that he was short in stature, which explains why he climbed up into a sycamore tree. But Jesus did not single out Zacchaeus because he was short or because he was in a tree. Jesus responded to Zacchaeus because He saw in him a need, a desire, a longing.

Zacchaeus was the chief tax collector in Jericho and worked for Rome. He was considered by his fellow Jews to be part of the evil oppression that had been placed upon the Jewish people by the Roman occupation forces. Tax collectors working for Rome often collected more than the tax due, and they often became very wealthy in the process of cheating others. Tax collectors were much despised and were considered to be great sinners.

John said about Jesus that He "knew all men, and had no need that anyone should testify of man, for He knew what was in man" (John 2:24–25). We find evidence of this a number of times in the Gospels when we read that Jesus knew the hearts of men or that He knew what people were thinking and attempting to do. Jesus *knew* Zacchaeus even though they had never met. He saw him as a man desperate for grace and the good news that God might forgive his sins, not as a man who cheated on his taxes.

☙ Think of a time when you discovered that someone was much different inside than you had always expected. What was your reaction when you discovered the "real person" inside? What had made you expect something different?

☙ When have you been surprised to learn that people misunderstood who you really were? What made them expect something different?

Awareness is the first step toward service. If you don't see people as Jesus sees them, you cannot minister to them as Jesus did. Before you can reach out to help someone, you must first see that person as having a need. Many people are so totally turned inward that they don't see others or hear their inner moaning and weeping. We all have problems, worries, temptations, and sorrows that nobody knows about.

One of the greatest stories in the Bible about awareness is found in Luke 8:42–48. Read that passage now, then consider the following questions:

&. Why do you suppose the woman touched Jesus "from behind" instead of speaking to Him face-to-face?

&. What were her expectations of Jesus? What might other people have expected from her?

You and I are called to become so sensitive to the needs of others that we *know* when someone is in need of healing and when they are reaching out to Jesus, even though they may not initially confess their need. We are to serve those in need with confidence and with confidentiality. Our sensitive service to them can cause them to touch Jesus with renewed faith and bring them healing.

Step 2: Availability

God is never too busy to hear the prayers of His people. Jesus was never too busy to respond to those who sought His help. When Jesus healed the woman who had had a flow of blood for 12 years, He was on His way to the home of a synagogue ruler named Jairus. Jairus' little girl had become extremely ill and was thought to be on her deathbed. Even so, Jesus stopped to heal someone who had reached out to Him with her faith. He had *time* for her.

When Jesus encountered Zacchaeus in Jericho, He was on His way to a final week of ministry in Jerusalem—a week that would culminate in His death on the cross and resurrection from the grave. Nothing was more important in the overall life of Jesus than His sacrificial death and resurrection from the dead. And yet, He had *time* for Zacchaeus.

The woman with a hemorrhage was considered to be unclean, an outcast in society. According to the religious Jews, this woman had no right to be in a crowd of people or to touch anyone, much less Jesus.

Zacchaeus was a hated tax collector, a sinner in the eyes of all who lived in Jericho. He, too, was a social outcast. And yet, Jesus made Himself available to both the hemorrhaging woman and the despised tax collector.

People today are starving for the gifts of time and concern. They are desperate for someone to listen to them or to pay attention to them. Sometimes those who need our time and attention the most are those who are held in very low esteem by society. Prisons, nursing homes, and hospitals for the mentally ill are filled with people who are lonely and forsaken, outcasts.

We must be available to people in need if we are to serve them as Jesus served.

> Let no one seek his own, but each one the other's well-being.

> —1 Corinthians 10:24

Think back over the past week. When did you have opportunities to set aside your own well-being in order to serve someone else? What did you do?

What situations might you face in the coming week where you can serve others?

Step 3: Acceptance

Jesus did not say to Zacchaeus, "Clean up your act. When you stop collecting taxes, I'll come to your house." He didn't say to the woman with a flow of blood, "As soon as you stop bleeding, come see Me." Jesus accepted both Zacchaeus and this woman just as they were.

Accepting others does not mean that we accept the way they are without intending to help change things for the better. It means accepting them the way that they are in order that we might help them move forward in their lives. Jesus did not leave Zacchaeus the same way He found him. Zacchaeus had a change of heart as the result of Jesus' going to his house. In His encounter with the woman who was hemorrhaging, Jesus healed her body *and* restored her to her community—He made her *whole*.

Our motivation must always be to serve people in Christ, to help them to become all that they can be as God's children. Acceptance is neither a denial of their current condition nor a belief that things can never improve for the person. We err greatly if we require others to "get good" before we help them "get God." God did not place any preconditions upon us before He forgave us generously. We therefore are in no position to place conditions upon others. We must accept them as they are and serve them just as we would serve the most righteous and highly esteemed person we know. This is the very essence of unconditional love.

> Heal the sick, cleanse the lepers, raise the dead, cast out demons. Freely you have received, freely give.
>
> —Matthew 10:8

What, besides your salvation, have you "freely received" from God?

☞. How can you share those gifts with others in service to Christ?

c∞ɔ

Step 4: Abiding

The Scriptures say that Jesus stayed at the house of Zacchaeus. He was there long enough for a meal, perhaps even an overnight stay. To serve others best, we must "abide" with them. We must walk in their shoes, see things through their eyes, be close enough to them and spend enough time with them to be of lasting benefit to them. Service is not a "hit-and-run" activity.

Jesus made earth His abode for about 30 years. God did not send His Son to deliver a quick 30-second message from a cloud in the sky. He sent Him to live among men and abide with them day in and day out, through all kinds of situations, so that they might truly see Him and know Him fully.

We are called to abide in Christ always—to be in such close relationship with Him and His Word that it is virtually impossible for others to tell where our love ends and His begins (John 8:31–32; 15:5). At the same time, we are to abide in loving relationship with others; we are to be the "body" of Christ. It is only when we serve others in this way that people can count on us to be there in a time of need. When we abide with others and remain available to them, our witness becomes truly strong and steadfast to them. The person who flits from ministry to ministry, church to church, job to job is far less effective than the person who puts down roots and chooses to *abide* in relationship with others.

🔖 Think of someone who has chosen to abide with you in steadfast friendship. How does it feel to have that kind of friend? In what ways do you serve one another?

One of the best examples of abiding is in the early church. When believers in Christ were ostracized by their families and friends, they banded together. Many of the new Christians lost their jobs, their inheritances, or their social standing. Rather than turn away from Christ, however, they turned toward Christ and toward one another, helping one another in very practical ways and forming a community of service that resulted in adequate provision for all (Acts 2:44–47). The result was a revival. As people saw how the new Christians loved and cared for one another, they were drawn to Christ as never before.

What was true then is true today. When unbelievers see Christians loving and serving one another and reaching out to others in need, they say, "I want to be a part of that group. I want what those people have."

> Now all who believed were together, and had all things in common, and sold their possessions and goods, and divided them among all, as anyone had need. So continuing daily with one accord in the temple, and breaking bread from house to house, they ate their food with gladness and simplicity of heart, praising God and having favor with all the people. And the Lord added to the church daily those who were being saved.
>
> —Acts 2:44-47

57

▸ What does it mean in practical terms to "have all things in common"? How can your church or Bible study group improve on this concept? How can you personally improve?

▸ What does it mean to "continue daily with one accord"? How well does your church or Bible study group do in this area? How might things improve?

Step 5: Abandonment

The ultimate step in service is self-abandonment—laying aside all of one's selfish desires and all of one's personal agenda in order to do whatever God asks.

Mary of Bethany broke her bottle of very costly oil of spikenard and poured it over Jesus' feet. She engaged in an act of self-abandonment. Nothing mattered to her but serving Jesus. When Jesus entered the home of Zacchaeus, He abandoned any concern for His public reputation. He knew that the majority of the people in Jericho would accuse Him of aligning with a sinner. He was willing to risk a loss of general public esteem in order to bring salvation to the household of Zacchaeus. Peter went to the house of Cornelius, abandoning years of prejudice against Gentiles. He was willing to go because it was clear to him that God was calling him to go, even if it meant stepping outside the bounds of his own "comfort zone" (Acts 10). Four men carried their paralyzed friend to Jesus on a stretcher and tore a hole in the roof in order to lower him into Jesus' presence when they couldn't get past the crowd in the doorway. They abandoned their own schedule, and their own desires. They let nothing stand in the way of helping their friend get to Jesus (Mark 2:1–12).

God calls us to abandon our concern for ourselves and to move outside ourselves in service to others. In so doing, we actually find ourselves and enter into the true meaning for our lives. Self-abandonment was the message that Jesus had for a rich young man who came to Him one day and asked, "Good Teacher, what shall I do that I may inherit eternal life?" Jesus reminded him of the commandments, which this man knew and had kept diligently. Being a good, religious man, however, was not enough. Jesus called him to a degree of abandonment in service. He said, "One thing you lack: Go your way, sell whatever you have and give to the poor, and you will have treasure in heaven; and come, take up the cross, and follow Me" (Mark 10:21). Utter abandonment to self is what Jesus required of this young man—it is also what He requires of us.

☙ How does this concept of "dying to self" compare with the teachings of the world around us? What do you think Jesus might say to those who teach us to pursue self-esteem and self-fulfillment?

...Assuredly, I say to you, there is no one who has left house or brothers or sisters or father or mother or wife or children or lands, for My sake and the gospel's, who shall not receive a hundredfold now in this time—houses and brothers and sisters and mothers and children and lands, with persecutions—and in the age to come, eternal life. But many who are first will be last, and the last first.

—Mark 10:29-31

_∞ Notice that Jesus adds "with persecutions" to the list of rewards for service. Why do His people receive persecution when they serve others?

_∞ When have you seen the principle of "the first shall be last" in real life? When have you *not* seen it work out that way?

Where Are You in Your Service?

Once again, the pattern toward full service is this: awareness, availability, acceptance, abiding, and abandonment. Where are you in your service? To what next step is God calling you?

You must be aware of the needs of others before you will ever make an effort to meet those needs. You must be available if you are to serve. You must accept others fully, just as they are, if you are to give them the unconditional love of Christ. It is as you abide with others over time that your service becomes steadfast and reliable, and your heart is knit to the hearts of others. Finally, the servant is called to exercise complete abandonment—not merely serving others some of the time, but living in a constant state of outreach to others at all times—on the job, at home, in the community, at church, and wherever God leads.

How well are you doing in these areas? In what ways might God be calling you to abandon yourself to others in service, or to abide with others more?

This is My commandment, that you love one another as I have loved you. Greater love has no one than this, than to lay down one's life for his friends.

—John 15:12-13

When have you been called upon to serve someone to the point where it felt like you were laying down your life for that person?

When has someone done that for you?

Let love be without hypocrisy. Abhor what is evil. Cling to what is good. Be kindly affectionate to one another with brotherly love, in honor giving preference to one another; not lagging in diligence, fervent in spirit, serving the Lord; rejoicing in hope, patient in tribulation, continuing steadfastly in prayer; distributing to the needs of the saints, given to hospitality.

—Romans 12:9-13

What does it mean to "let love be without hypocrisy"? When has your love for others been tainted with hypocrisy? How can you prevent that in the future?

Give some hypothetical examples (not real people) of how you might encounter someone whose "evil" you should "abhor" while still clinging to what is good. How does a person distinguish between these things?

Today and Tomorrow

TODAY: JESUS DEMONSTRATED THAT SERVICE REQUIRES AWARENESS, AVAILABILITY, ACCEPTANCE, ABIDING, AND ABANDONMENT.

TOMORROW: I WILL ASK GOD TO SHOW ME AREAS IN MY LIFE WHERE I NEED TO STRENGTHEN ONE OR MORE OF THESE PRINCIPLES.

The Qualities of an Effective Servant

Part 1

❧ In This Lesson ☙

LEARNING: WHAT ARE THE QUALITIES OF AN EFFECTIVE SERVANT?

GROWING: WHERE WILL I GET THESE QUALITIES, IF I DON'T HAVE THEM ALREADY?

The early church grew rapidly after the ascension of Jesus. The Hellenists (Greek-influenced Christians) began to complain that the widows of the Hebrews (Orthodox Christians) were being shown favoritism at the communal meals held daily by the church. The 12 apostles called a meeting of a large number of the Christian disciples in the city.

Read about it now in Acts 6:5–6.

Seven men were commissioned for a very specific role in the church. It was not the same role as that of the apostles, but it nevertheless was a vital *ministry* role within the church. These seven men became the first deacons. The word for *deacon* in the Greek language had a much different meaning from the meaning of the word today in most Christian denominations. In many of our churches today, deacons are chosen for their business ability and their position in the world. Once elected as deacons, they often attempt to fill spiritual roles of leadership.

The first deacons, however, represent an almost 180-degree difference in role. They were chosen for spiritual qualities, not "professional" qualities, and they were given very practical roles of service. They were not rulers, per se.

The word for *deacon* is also used in the Greek language to literally express the concepts "to run, to hasten." The first deacons were expected to be quick in their response to the needs of believers. They were given the job of protecting the harmony of the fellowship—of making sure that things were done equitably and in order, of making certain that all the needs were met, and of ensuring that no clique groups developed within the body of Christ.

The first deacons were chosen on the basis of six qualities in their lives: They were submissive, of good reputation, full of the Holy Spirit, had wisdom, had vision for the work of God, and demonstrated humility. These are the same qualities that today make the most effective servants.

✎ Consider the qualities of deacons: submissive, good reputation, filled with the Holy Spirit, wise, committed to God's work, and humble. How many of these qualities do others see in your life?

The Quality of Submissiveness

The deacons were under the authority of apostles. The apostles were the ones who laid hands upon the deacons, prayed for them, and imparted to them their authority within the church. In many churches today, this process has been turned upside down—the deacons are the ones who call the pastors and then lay hands on them and commission them to serve their local church. The original order established in the first-century church is far more effective and, more importantly, it is *God's* design.

The apostles were the ones who devoted themselves to prayer and the ministry of the Word. They were the ones who preached the gospel of Jesus to those who were not yet a part of the fellowship of Christians, and they no doubt were the ones who baptized the new converts upon their acceptance of Christ. *Apostle* literally means "one sent out," and the apostles filled this role—they were at the cutting edge of the outreach of the church.

The role of the deacons was turned inward toward the believers—they were responsible for running the practical matters in the church. They were men of prayer and students of God's Word, but prayer and preaching were not their primary responsibilities. This does not mean that on occasion a deacon might not speak publicly. Stephen is described in the Scriptures as a man "full of faith and power" who "did great wonders and signs among the people" (Acts 6:8). He became the first martyr as the result of his speaking boldly about Jesus to the Jewish religious council. He did not, however, have preaching and prayer as his job description. He exercised his spiritual gifts in the office of deacon; his primary role was to oversee the meeting of practical needs, not to set the spiritual agenda for the church.

An effective servant is one who *always* submits his will to those who are in authority over him. We each are in a line of authority; no person lives without having someone in authority over him. Ultimately, that authority is Christ Jesus. It is only when we learn to submit our wills to His will and to obey those whom God has placed over us that we truly can be effective servants.

A rebellious person might go through some of the external motions of service for a period of time, but he will not *remain* a steadfast servant over time. A rebellious person cannot be truly effective in helping people grow in their faith or experience an increasing reliance upon the Holy Spirit because the rebellious person is not totally reliant upon the Holy Spirit himself.

Submission is not a state of groveling or of weakness, as we tend to think in our modern culture. Rather, it is recognizing that someone has greater God-given authority in a particular situation. It is yielding one's decision-making power to a higher authority, curbing one's behavior to conform to the rule established by one who occupies a position of authority.

&. How do you feel when you submit yourself to a person in authority?

&. When have you experienced a real sense of peace because you knew that someone else was taking care of difficulties?

Submissiveness and faith are closely linked. If you fail to believe that God is going to provide for you, protect you, or work things for good on your behalf, you are unlikely to submit to God or trust Him. If you believe that God is your heavenly Father and that all He does is ultimately for your blessing and eternal good, then you are likely to submit to Him and to have faith in Him, trusting Him for every detail of your life.

The first deacons were willing to let the apostles be apostles and to take on their own role of service as deacons. They did not try to lead the church, but they tried to resolve the problems within the church under the authority granted to them by the apostles.

As servants today, we are not called to make our own spiritual decisions, but to submit ourselves to the Holy Spirit and to do only what He directs us to say and do. Having a submissive spirit is important regardless of a person's rank or position. A senior pastor or denominational leader must be no less submissive in spirit than the newest convert to Christ. The position that one holds does not alter the state that must exist in one's heart. Jesus recognized a Roman centurion as being one of the most submissive and faith-filled people that He encountered during His ministry.

Read Matt. 8:5–13 now and consider the following questions:

∝ Why do you think the Centurion said that he was "not worthy" to have Jesus enter his house? What leadership quality does this man's attitude demonstrate?

‌ Why did Jesus proclaim that the Centurion had great faith, based upon what the Centurion had said? What element of faith did he reveal in his words?

‌

The Quality of a Good Reputation

The deacons were chosen first and foremost because they were "men of good reputation." They had exemplary character and were men of the highest integrity. A good reputation is something that we are to work at achieving and to value highly. A "good name" is a tremendous asset. Having a good reputation does not mean that people will totally agree with you at all times. You may disagree with the decisions made by a person of good character and still admire and respect a person as a man of God.

From the biblical point of view, goodness and godliness are the same. One cannot bear a reputation for goodness without being godly; a godly person is good. Goodness is one of the qualities of the Holy Spirit that we are to bear as His fruit in our lives (Gal. 5:22).

People judge a person's reputation on the basis of what that person says and does. The fact is, what you believe is inevitably revealed by what you say, and what you say inevitably dictates what you do. If a person believes God's Word, says that he is making God's Word his way of life, and then truly attempts to live out God's Word on a daily basis, that person is building a good reputation.

A good reputation has nothing to do with the standards of success established by the world. Being rich, famous, or the leader of an organization does not necessarily make a person good or godly. The lowliest wage earner can be a person of excellent reputation. The most unrecognized person within the church might still be a person about whom all say, "That is a godly person."

Why is a good reputation so vital for service? Because genuine service is a reflection of God's love and presence. If a person is going through the motions of service with an evil intent or a selfish interest, others will know it. The person serving will be suspect, and even the service itself will be suspect. In our culture today, many think that a person's character doesn't matter as long as the outcome of his work is good. From God's standpoint, the character of the person giving the service *is* what makes the outcome of that person's work good. You cannot separate inner character and outer deeds. In the end, a good reputation is vital to good service.

A person's reputation is one of the foremost factors in his witness to the world about the saving grace of God. A person's greatest witness for Christ is found in the way that he lives his daily life. Who you are, from the inside out, is the platform on which you give service. Your service will not redeem you or make your reputation. Your reputation for having a godly character is what will redeem your service and give you a witness for Christ Jesus.

We must also be aware that a good reputation does not necessarily spare a person from persecution (2 Tim. 3:12–15). Those who perform good service to others sometimes are criticized for it, misunderstood because of it, or ridiculed as being a "goody two-shoes." What can be said for a good reputation, however, is that it survives persecution—even if that persecution leads to death. A good reputation lasts, and it affects others for good. If a person's reputation is a godly one in Christ Jesus, it will last into eternity.

If you want your service to outlive your lifetime and be credited to your eternal reward, you must be a person who strives to achieve and maintain a good reputation. Don't be discouraged if you face persecution or if your reputation is assaulted for the service that you perform. Press on. Your reputation *will* be vindicated eventually, and your service *will* be rewarded by God.

⚬ How do you feel if a "bad person" does a good thing for you? What is likely to be your response to the person, and to the service that he rendered to you?

> ...every good tree bears good fruit, but a bad tree bears bad fruit. A good tree cannot bear bad fruit, nor can a bad tree bear good fruit.
>
> —Matthew 7:17-18

⚬ What does "bad fruit" taste like? How does this image of bad-tasting fruit compare with acts of service given by someone with mixed motives?

🙛 Jesus tells us that a good tree cannot bear bad fruit. What does that suggest about the importance of godliness in our lives, as we seek to serve others?

The Quality of Being Full of the Holy Spirit

The apostles requested that the members of the Jerusalem church choose as deacons men who were "full of the Holy Spirit" (Acts 6:3). The Holy Spirit is the One who guides Christians into good words, good works, and a good walk before our heavenly Father. He is the One who enables us to perform good works that have a lasting benefit to the kingdom of God. It is virtually impossible to do anything on this earth that is of eternal value unless one is enabled by the Holy Spirit to do that work.

God alone knows which of your works has the potential to be the most effective and productive in His kingdom. He alone guarantees that your work will succeed, in spite of persecution and your own failures. God alone can cause a work of service to become a point of witness to a lost soul and can use your service to redeem lives for all eternity. God alone can assure you of an eternal reward for your service. Without God, nothing that you do can be remotely as important, beneficial, or lasting as what you do *with* God.

We already mentioned Stephen as a man who was "full of faith and the Holy Spirit" and "full of faith and power" (Acts 6:5, 8). What an amazing and wonderful reputation to have! To be *full* of God's Spirit means that Stephen's life was overflowing and continuously demonstrating the character of God. He was a man who embodied all of the fruit of the Spirit described by Paul: love, joy, peace, longsuffering, kindness, goodness, faithfulness, gentleness, and self-control (Gal. 5:22–23). Paul also wrote that there is nothing in the law — either God's law or man's law — that prohibits a person from having these traits. They are qualities of character that are desirable in *all* people, in *all* periods of history, and in young and old alike.

A servant who is full of the Holy Spirit is like Jesus, who was full of the Holy Spirit from the moment of His birth. A person filled with the Holy Spirit is one who says what Jesus would say in any situation, do what Jesus would do in any circumstance, and live as Jesus would live in any environment.

A servant who is full of the Holy Spirit is obviously one who is completely submissive to the Holy Spirit for direction, guidance, and power. He does nothing that the Holy Spirit does not prompt and enable. He is totally reliant upon God for every move that he makes.

Christians often say to one another, "If only Jesus were here, He'd remedy this situation." The fact is, if we are truly full of the same Holy Spirit that filled Jesus, then it's as if Jesus is in our midst. And our collective service or ministry to others will be just as effective and meaningful as if that person were touched by the very hands of Christ Jesus, heard the very words of Christ Jesus, or received the very gifts that Christ Jesus would give.

When we attempt to serve others without relying upon the Holy Spirit, we burn out, become discouraged at failures and persecutions, and often become lax in our service and weak in our desire to serve. None of us can remain faithful, devoted, and consistent in our service without the Holy Spirit's help. To be truly effective in your service to others, you must ask the Holy Spirit to work in you and through you—today, tomorrow, and every day in your future.

🍃 When have you attempted to do a "good work" without relying upon the Holy Spirit? What were the long-range results—in you, as well as in those you served?

🍃 When have you been completely reliant upon the Holy Spirit in your service? What were the long-range results—in you, and in those you served?

But the fruit of the Spirit is love, joy, peace, longsuffering, kindness, goodness, faithfulness, gentleness, self-control. Against such there is no law.

—Galatians 5:22-23

◈ Define each of the fruit of the Spirit below, and assess how much each is evident in your own life:

Love:

Joy:

Peace:

Longsuffering:

Kindness:

Goodness:

Faithfulness:

Gentleness:

Self-control:

Therefore submit yourselves to every ordinance of man for the Lord's sake, whether to the king as supreme, or to governors, as to those who are sent by him for the punishment of evildoers and for the praise of those who do good. For this is the will of God, that by doing good you may put to silence the ignorance of foolish men—as free, yet not using liberty as a cloak for vice, but as bondservants of God.

—1 Peter 2:13-16

∼ According to this passage, for what purposes has God ordained authority in human society?

∼ How does this compare with modern attitudes toward the functions of government?

∼ Today and Tomorrow ∼

TODAY: AN EFFECTIVE SERVANT IS FIRST AND FOREMOST FILLED WITH THE PRESENCE OF THE HOLY SPIRIT.

TOMORROW: I WILL PRAYERFULLY STRIVE TO STRENGTHEN THE FRUIT OF THE SPIRIT IN MY OWN LIFE.

The Qualities of an Effective Servant

Part 2

LEARNING: How do wisdom, vision, and humility affect my service?

GROWING: Where do those qualities come from?

〰️

In the last lesson, we covered three of the traits that deacons are to embody in their service: submissiveness, a good reputation, and a life filled with the Holy Spirit. In this lesson, we will cover the remaining traits that are vital for an effective servant of God's people.

These character-trait qualities are identified as the qualities of effective service within the church, but they are also the qualities that are most effective in serving others in order to bring them to Christ. A godly person who simultaneously has a submissive human spirit and is filled with the power of the Holy Spirit is an extremely effective witness for Christ. Such a person is a "model believer," a man or woman who has a tremendous role in the growth and development of God's kingdom. Show me a godly janitor who is submissive and filled with God's Holy Spirit, and I will show you a person who truly makes a lasting difference for good. Show me a senior pastor who has an "I-can-do-it-on-my-own" attitude and who is not reliant upon the Holy Spirit, and I will show you a person who is probably in error in various areas of his

76

personal life. His reputation, his attitude, and his lack of the fruit of the Holy Spirit in his life will eventually harm the church.

No matter what job you hold, you are called to be a servant who embodies the character traits that were required of the first deacons. If you are to serve others and do so effectively, then you must bear the same spiritual integrity that they manifested.

The Quality of Wisdom

The first deacons chosen by the church were to be men who were full of wisdom (Acts 6:3). Wisdom is knowing both what God desires a person to do and how God desires the job to be done, and then having the courage actually to *do* what is required. Stated another way: What a person does and the degree to which his actions are successful are a measure of that person's wisdom.

You cannot be wise and say nothing or do nothing. How will anybody know that you are wise? How will *you* know that you are wise? Wisdom is not simply having head knowledge. It is having *application* knowledge—knowing how, when, and where to apply one's knowledge of God's purposes, plans, and commandments. Wisdom is knowledge that is lived out, acted upon, and made useful to real-life decisions.

Wisdom comes from God. It flows from the Holy Spirit to us as we rely upon the Holy Spirit for it. God doesn't pour out His wisdom on people who don't want it or request it. At the same time, He is more than willing to pour out His wisdom in generous portions on those who do desire it and ask for it. If you want more wisdom, ask God to give it to you!

Wisdom is vital for service and especially for service in the church, because without it *God's* answer to human problems is not discernible. Service can be rendered solely from fleshly desires and from human levels of intelligence and ability, but such service is limited and often in error. Can you imagine what might have happened if the early church had simply chosen the smartest men that they knew, but not necessarily the wisest men that they knew? They would have had a catastrophe because they would have had seven highly "intelligent" opinions about how to serve and what to do, but no consensus in the Spirit and no true unity in purpose, plan, or result.

When have you been the victim of someone's "bright idea"—that turned out not to be what the Holy Spirit desired?

When have you acted upon a "bright idea" of your own—only to discover later that it wasn't wise?

Wisdom is something that we need on a daily basis. Ask the Holy Spirit every morning to give you the wisdom that you will need to deal with the circumstances and situations that you will face in the coming day. As you face particular decisions, ask the Holy Spirit to guide you. As you encounter people throughout your day, ask the Holy Spirit to direct your conversation. You can never ask too much or too often for God's wisdom.

We must ask for wisdom in faith (James 1:6). After you have prayed for wisdom, make the decision or take the action that you believe God has called you to do. Don't second-guess God or yourself at that point. God will reveal to you if you have erred. The only way to grow in your ability to apply God's Word effectively is to obey what God's Word says. Keep in mind always that the Holy Spirit will never direct you to do something that is contrary to God's Word, the Bible.

> If any of you lacks wisdom, let him ask of God, who gives to all liberally and without reproach, and it will be given to him. But let him ask in faith, with no doubting, for he who doubts is like a wave of the sea driven and tossed by the wind.

> —James 1:5-6

Describe how a "doubting" man might be like a wave of the sea.

> The fear of the Lord is the beginning of wisdom, And the knowledge of the Holy One is understanding.

> —Proverbs 9:10

What is the "fear of the Lord"? What does it look like when it is part of our lives?

The Quality of Vision

The deacons chosen by the early church were men who had a vision for what God desired to be done in their midst. They were not attempting to fulfill their own desires or goals but the desires of God's heart for His people. True service always has an evangelistic, outward reach to it that is borne of a vision for what God desires to do on the earth. We each are responsible for winning as many people as possible to Christ Jesus in our generation. When we have this at the core of our desire to serve, everything that we do takes on greater meaning.

A person with a vision for the greater plans and purposes of God is a person who finds meaning and fulfillment in even the most mundane of tasks. For example, we are not to feed people simply to feed people. We are to feed the hungry so that, with full stomachs, they might fully receive the gospel of Christ. We are not to provide clothing, shelter, or medical help to people merely so that they can be warm and live longer. We are to engage in these forms of service so that people might not have any practical, material, or physical barriers that keep them from hearing God's call of grace and forgiveness to them. True Christian service involves removing the obstacles that keep a person from having "ears to hear" and "eyes to see."

Without very practical, daily service being performed by the deacons in the early church, it is very likely that large numbers of needy Christians would have fallen away from their newfound faith. The Christian life would simply have been too difficult for them—their needs would have loomed so large that they would not have been able to hear the full message of the gospel.

A vision grows in us when we ask ourselves *why* God has called us to help others. We see the bigger picture: God desires to meet the needs of all people and to show His love to us in practical, tangible ways. God blesses His people materially, practically, and physically as much as He blesses His people spiritually. So often we place such great importance upon God's spiritual blessing that we neglect to give importance to God's material blessings to those who are lacking the basics necessary for life. Jesus said that He came not only to give us eternal life but an abundant life in the here and now (John 10:10). As His servants, we are to provide service that leads both to an abundant life on this earth and to a spiritual life that is everlasting.

One form of service is not to be replaced by the other. We are to have a vision for the greater service—leading a person to Christ—as we engage diligently in performing the practical service of meeting daily needs.

෴ What is your reaction to people who are "so heavenly minded that they are of little earthly good"?

> If I do not do the works of My Father, do not believe Me; but if I do, though you do not believe Me, believe the works, that you may know and believe that the Father is in Me, and I in Him."
>
> —John 10:37-38

෴ What "works of the Father" did Jesus perform in His earthly ministry?

✍ How did Jesus' works of service to others prove to the people around Him that He was doing God's work?

⌘

The Quality of Humility

Perhaps the supreme character trait of the first-century deacons was humility. These men were filled with faith and power, they had a vision for God's work, and they had outstanding reputations—yet they were asked to *serve tables*. They were asked to become, in effect, waiters. They were responsible for making certain that everyone at the church's communal meals received enough food and that their needs were met without prejudice or favoritism.

Many of the most important roles in the church today are roles similar to that of serving tables. Show me ushers, greeters, parking attendants, hospitality hostesses, and janitors who do their work with the same spirit as that of the first deacons, and I will show you a church that is headed for great effectiveness in the winning of souls and the building up of the body of Christ.

Humility is at the foundation of submissiveness. It is the complement to wisdom—it is what keeps the wise from becoming arrogant. Humility is a sign of being filled with the Holy Spirit; it is a hallmark among those who have good reputations. Humility says, "Not my will, but Your will;" it is the trait that opens one's eyes to the broader vision that God has for a human life.

Humility will cause a person to see every task as a "job" to be done for God, rather than as a "position" to be filled to win the approval of men. In serving tables, the deacons had this as their goal: "See that everybody is taken care of." Seeing that everybody is taken care of is one of the best definitions of service that I have ever heard. When we serve an individual, we are actually serving the greater body of Christ. Any form of service that we desire to render to the church as a whole must first be done for an individual.

It is not enough that a person be fed once. A person must be fed consistently so that hunger is no longer a part of his daily concern. It is not enough that a person be greeted warmly on one Sunday a year. A person must feel welcome within the church body every time he sets foot inside the church or encounters a member of the church. It is not enough that a person be told the gospel once. A person must be presented with the gospel at all times—in every word, by every deed, and through every action that is taken on his behalf. Humility calls us to see the *person* who needs our help, not the crowd who might shower adoration upon us.

Pride and service are incompatible. Compare the two:

Pride:	Service:
Self-seeking	Seeks out the best for others
Insists on having my own way	Makes a way for others
Demands recognition	Works for results
Fills us up with self-importance	Empties us of self

If we are willing to bow our knees before God, we must also be willing to get down on our knees to help others. Humility before God must extend to our having a humble spirit before men.

⌒∞⌒

Likewise you younger people, submit yourselves to your elders. Yes, all of you be submissive to one another, and be clothed with humility, for "God resists the proud, but gives grace to the humble." Therefore humble yourselves under the mighty hand of God, that He may exalt you in due time.

—1 Peter 5:5-6

What does it mean to be "clothed with humility"? How is this different from being clothed with pride?

How does a person humble himself "under the mighty hand of God"?

The Result of Genuine Service

Acts 6:7 tells us the result of the church's choosing deacons who bore these six qualities: submissiveness, good reputation, full of the Holy Spirit, wisdom, a vision for the work of God, and humility:

> The word of God spread, and the number of the disciples multiplied greatly in Jerusalem, and a great many of the priests were obedient to the faith.

A church that is filled with people who are active in their service one to another is a church that is like a great magnet to lost souls. The reputation of that church spreads quickly. Christ is lifted up on the shoulders of men and women who are kneeling to perform good service to others. He draws the lost to Himself through the extended arms of believers.

Note that "a great many of the *priests* became obedient to the faith." The service of the deacons became an example to the believers. They, in turn, began to serve one another with generous, humble, submissive spirits that were open to the Holy Spirit's wisdom and power. As the believers began to serve, the world took notice. The entire atmosphere of Jerusalem changed. Many of those who were engaged in the priestly functions of the temple actually began to claim Jesus as Messiah.

If you want to bring joy to the heart of your pastor today, begin to serve others in your church as if you are serving Jesus Himself. Pour out your love to your fellow believers. Your example will draw unbelievers to your church fellowship, and your pastor will be encouraged as never before. You'll see a change in the way that he preaches, teaches, and leads your congregation. Nothing warms the heart of a pastor more than to see those in his congregation loving one another.

If you want to see church growth, begin with service. It flows automatically from hearts that bear the qualities of submissiveness, godly character, wisdom, a vision for God's work, humility, and a desire to be filled to overflowing with God's Spirit.

∂. In what ways are you feeling challenged to serve others as the first-century deacons did?

> But if you have bitter envy and self-seeking in your hearts, do not boast and lie against the truth. This wisdom does not descend from above, but is earthly, sensual, demonic. For where envy and self-seeking exist, confusion and every evil thing are there. But the wisdom that is from above is first pure, then peaceable, gentle, willing to yield, full of mercy and good fruits, without partiality and without hypocrisy.
>
> —James 3:14-17

∂. Give some examples of worldly "wisdom" which proves that it is "earthly, sensual, demonic".

🔊 Put each of the following characteristics of true wisdom into your own words:

Pure:

Peaceable:

Gentle:

Willing to yield:

Full of mercy:

Full of good fruits:

Without partiality:

Without hypocrisy:

🔊 Today and Tomorrow 🔊

TODAY: THE FIRST-CENTURY DEACONS WERE MEN OF WISDOM, HUMILITY, AND VISION.

TOMORROW: I WILL SEEK THE HOLY SPIRIT'S HELP IN DEVELOPING THESE VITAL QUALITIES THIS WEEK.

LESSON 8

Equipped for Service

❧ In This Lesson ❧

LEARNING: BUT WHAT IF I DON'T *HAVE* ANY GIFTS? AND WHAT IF *I'M* THE ONE WHO NEEDS COMFORTING?

GROWING: HOW CAN I USE MY OWN EXPERIENCES TO SERVE OTHERS?

People offer any number of excuses for not engaging in active service to others. Some say that they don't have time; others say that they have other priorities. The two basic reasons, however, at the *root* of why people don't serve are these:

1. *Pride.* They simply don't want to humble themselves to serve others. Selfishness is a form of pride—people don't want to be inconvenienced or detoured from what they want to do, when they want to do it. Self-centeredness is pride.

2. *Fear of failure.* Many people feel that they don't have anything to give to others or that others will not be open to receiving what they can offer.

☙ *The person who steadfastly refuses to engage in service is a person who doesn't understand who God is.* If a person truly has an understanding of God as a loving, generous Father—One who gave His only begotten Son so that we might be reconciled to Him and live with Him forever—then he will have a built-in desire to give. How can a person know the extent of God's love and not want to share it with others? God not only requires us to give service, He *desires* for us to give service. If we know that God is love, then we must also know that we must love others, since God's Spirit resides within us. That means serving others and giving to others in order to meet their needs.

☙ *The person who steadfastly refuses to engage in service is a person who doesn't understand why he is alive.* So many people today question, "Why am I here?" The Christian should never have to ask that question. If you are a follower of Jesus Christ, you are alive on this earth to worship God and to reflect glory to God by the way you serve your fellow man. Loving God and loving others, just as you love your own life, is God's commandment to you. It is your purpose, your role, your meaning in life.

☙ *The person who steadfastly refuses to engage in service is a person who doesn't understand God's purpose for this world.* God's purpose for the world is that all men might come to know Him and receive forgiveness through Christ Jesus. Jesus came to seek and to save *all* who are lost. God's purpose for you as a part of the larger body of Christ is that you be a part of an ongoing, consistent effort to win lost souls to Christ and to build up the faith of your fellow Christians. God's purpose is that His kingdom be established on earth, just as it is in heaven. Jesus taught us to pray, "Our Father in heaven, hallowed be Your name. Your kingdom come. Your will be done on earth as it is in heaven" (Matt. 6:9–10).

If a person truly understands who God is, why he is on this earth, and what God's purposes are for all mankind, how can he dare to say to God, "I'd rather do my own thing than serve You by serving others"? How does he dare to exert his own will over God's will?

I have much more compassion for those who don't believe that they have any talents to give to God than I have for those who know that they are talented and yet refuse to use their talents for God's glory. My word to those of you who believe that you don't have anything to offer in the way of service is this: *You do.* God does not call any person to do anything within His kingdom unless He also equips that person—spiritually, materially, physically, financially, and in all other ways. Whatever type of service God may be opening up to you, He has prepared you and equipped you to succeed in doing it, and He will continue to assist you and increase your talents as you engage in the work set before you.

&. How would life be different if God's will were done on earth to the same degree that it is in heaven? How would your life be different?

⌐❈¬

Created for Service

Service is a part of God's reason for creating you. Ephesians 2:10 tells us:

> We are His workmanship, created in Christ Jesus for good works, which God prepared beforehand that we should walk in them.

Even before you were born, God had in mind who you would be and what He would have you do in this very specific time right now. You haven't arrived where you are in your life by accident or whim. God's plan and purpose for you are unfolding. God would not have you engage in service for Him without preparing you for the challenge.

Your service is an outgrowth of the talents and abilities that God has placed in your life. We each have been given certain "service-ready equipment" from birth: a unique personality, mental and emotional capacities, talents, and strengths.

God has been at work in your life from your first moments, molding and preparing you to fulfill His plan and purpose for you. Throughout our lives, God has allowed us to have certain experiences, engage in certain relationships, and be a part of certain groups of people in certain environments and cultures—all of which become a part of the mix of who we are and what we bring to any form of ministry or service. We can be assured that He will continue to work in us until the day we die. God works in us and through us as we serve, and He uses our service to prepare us for even greater service in the days ahead.

You may feel that you are at the kindergarten level of service—that you have limited resources and abilities with which to serve. God's plan is that you use what you have been given to the fullest and, as you use those abilities, He will *increase* them so that you are able to serve Him with greater abilities. God's purpose for you in service is never to decrease you but to increase you and to cause you to prosper in all areas of your life—mentally, physically, emotionally, materially, and above all, spiritually.

 What talents and skills has God given you? How can those skills be used to serve others?

    ...He who has begun a good work in you will complete it until
    the day of Jesus Christ.

                                        —Philippians 1:6

 Notice that God will complete His work in us "*until* the day of Jesus Christ," rather than "*by* the day of Jesus Christ." What does this suggest about God's involvement in our lives?

๛ What does this suggest about our part in God's perfecting work?

Equipped with Spiritual Gifts

Not only have you been equipped with certain natural gifts and abilities, but the Holy Spirit dwells within you. He brings to you His unlimited gifts and abilities! That's why Paul could claim so boldly, "I can do all things through Christ who strengthens me" (Phil. 4:13). What you lack, the Holy Spirit supplies. When you are weak, He is strong. When you fail in your service to others, He has the capacity to continue to work all things together for good—both to you and to those whom you serve (Rom. 8:28). Indeed, if God is for us, who can be against us (Rom. 8:31)? We are guaranteed to be successful in our service to others as long as we rely upon the Holy Spirit to work in us, through us, and on our behalf—both individually and as members of the greater body of Christ.

In Romans 12:6–8, Paul cites several types of gifts that the Holy Spirit gives freely to those who believe in Christ Jesus:

Having then gifts differing according to the grace that is given to us, let us use them: if prophecy, let us prophesy in proportion to our faith; or ministry, let us use it in our ministering; he who teaches, in teaching; he who exhorts, in exhortation; he who gives, with liberality; he who leads, with diligence; he who shows mercy, with cheerfulness.

Note that Paul's emphasis is on the *use* of spiritual gifts. What the Holy Spirit gives to us we are to *use* for the benefit of others. They are not given to us for our exclusive benefit; they are given so that others might benefit and, in the process, we might grow in our faith and spiritual power. Furthermore, it is the Holy Spirit who determines which gift of *His* He will choose to put into operation at any given time in our lives and service to others. The gifts of the Spirit are just that—the Spirit's gifts. They reside in Him and are given to us for the greater use of the entire body of Christ. We see this clearly as Paul describes some of the gifts in 1 Corinthians 12:4–11:

> There are diversities of gifts, but the same Spirit. There are differences of ministries, but the same Lord. And there are diversities of activities, but it is the same God who works all in all. But the manifestation of the Spirit is given to each one for the profit of all: for to one is given the word of wisdom through the Spirit, to another the word of knowledge through the same Spirit, to another faith by the same Spirit, to another gifts of healings by the same Spirit, to another the working of miracles, to another prophecy, to another discerning of spirits, to another different kinds of tongues, to another the interpretation of tongues. But one and the same Spirit works all these things, distributing to each one individually as He wills.

God gives us supernatural gifts so that we might serve others. If you feel a need in your service to another person, ask God to endow you with whatever gift you need in order to get *His* job done for *His* glory. He will do so! He is the One who gives spiritual gifts so that His people might be edified and His kingdom expanded and His love and grace revealed to the lost.

⚜

Now may He who supplies seed to the sower, and bread for food, supply and multiply the seed you have sown and increase the fruits of your righteousness, while you are enriched in everything for all liberality, which causes thanksgiving through us to God.

—2 Corinthians 9:10-11

🐟 According to these verses, who is responsible for creating the "seed" of service to others? Who is responsible for sowing that seed?

🐟 What benefit does the sower receive for sowing the seed? What is the *purpose* of that benefit to the sower?

The Purpose of Gifts

Paul wrote this to the Corinthians (2 Cor. 1:3–4):

> Blessed be the God and Father of our Lord Jesus Christ, the Father of mercies and God of all comfort, who comforts us in all our tribulation, that we may be able to comfort those who are in any trouble, with the comfort with which we ourselves are comforted by God.

The gifts of the Holy Spirit are intended for us to use in comforting those who are in trouble. As we have been comforted by Christ, so we are to comfort others.

All of our experiences in life—and especially those which have brought us pain, sorrow, and suffering—equip us in unique ways to have empathy with others and to show compassion to them. Everything in your life—even your failures and suffering—has prepared you to show the love of God to others. God's grace to you in your times of suffering prepares you to become an effective minister of God to those who are currently suffering.

Too often, the laymen in a church expect the pastor to do all of the ministering to those who have emotional or spiritual needs. That is far from what the Bible sets as the standard for service. Read what Paul wrote to the Ephesians (Eph. 4:7, 11–13):

> To each one of us grace was given according to the measure of Christ's gift ... And He Himself gave some to be apostles, some prophets, some evangelists, and some pastors and teachers, for the equipping of the saints for the work of ministry, for the edifying of the body of Christ, till we all come to the unity of the faith and of the knowledge of the Son of God, to a perfect man, to the measure of the stature of the fullness of Christ.

The leaders in any church setting are placed there for one main reason: *to equip the saints for the work of ministry.* If you are a layman, you are a saint who is being equipped for ministry. Your purpose in life is not to listen to hundreds of sermons and attend dozens of seminars and then die and go to heaven. Your purpose is to hear the Word of God as it is preached and taught to you and then immediately and consistently to apply that preaching and teaching in practical forms of service to the people around you. The "work" of ministry belongs to all of God's people. In ministering to others, you become an agent of God's comfort and care.

⟶ According to 2 Cor. 1:3–4 (quoted above), why does God comfort us in our times of affliction?

⟶ How might this fact change your view of suffering?

It is out of thanksgiving for what God has done that we serve others. If you have been forgiven by God and are the recipient of God's love, then you *are* equipped for service. He will provide what you lack in ability.

⚬∞⚬

> For it is God who works in you both to will and to do for His good pleasure.
>
> —Philippians 2:13

⚫ According to this verse, what effect does God's will have upon our will and desires when we are in fellowship with Him?

⚫ How might this relationship with God's will require us to change our own plans sometimes?

⚫ Today and Tomorrow ⚫

TODAY: GOD SENDS EVERYTHING INTO MY LIFE—EVEN SORROW—FOR THE PURPOSE OF SERVING OTHERS.

TOMORROW: I WILL ASK GOD TO SHOW ME THIS WEEK HOW I CAN USE MY OWN LIFE EXPERIENCES TO SERVE OTHERS.

⚬∞⚬

LESSON 9

Five Principles of Successful Service

─────── ❧ **In This Lesson** ❧ ───────

LEARNING: HOW DO I DETERMINE THE SUCCESS AND RESULTS OF MY OWN
SERVICE?

GROWING: WHO AM I SUPPOSED TO BE SERVING?

─────── ∞ ───────

Service is a theme that runs throughout God's Word. The Bible is filled with countless examples of God's service to His people, ways in which God's people served God and others, and commandments that are related to service. In this lesson, we are going to take a look at five principles from God's Word that are related to service. These principles are interrelated and should be taken as a whole. God has made it very clear in His Word that He *requires* service from us. Service is not an option or a suggestion. It is a commandment.

Service is also our way to increased blessing and fulfillment in life. God does not command us to serve so that we might be diminished or made to suffer. Rather, God commands us to service so that He might reward us, bring us blessing, teach us, and develop a closer relationship with us. God always rewards our service with more of His presence and power and, ultimately, with eternal rewards that are beyond our ability to imagine.

Jesus said, "A servant is not greater than his master; nor is he who is sent greater than he who sent him. If you know these things, blessed are you if you do them" (John 13:16–17). We *must* serve. But this is a command that we should delight in obeying because service always reaps benefit—to us personally as well as to those whom we serve.

⤳ How do you feel about the fact that God commands service? How do you feel about the fact that God rewards service?

⸎

Principle 1: Volunteerism

A true servant doesn't wait to be asked. He discerns a need and acts decisively to meet it. A servant has a sensitive heart and a willing spirit. A volunteer is motivated by love and prompted to action by the presence of a need. A volunteer is *not* motivated by convenience or leisure time. Those who say "someday I'll get involved" or "someday I'll serve God" are offering lame excuses. If you are waiting for a convenient time to serve, you will never serve.

Ask yourself, "What is it that I won't do for God? What is it that I wouldn't do for another person?" An honest answer to those two questions will reveal your own self-pride. Jesus died naked, bloody, and battered, on a cross that was next to a public highway. He was made a laughingstock—a crown of thorns pressed into His brow and a sign above His head mocking Him as "King of the Jews." Jesus died for *your* sake so that you might have a Savior.

Furthermore, Jesus went to the cross voluntarily. The Bible gives us these words of Jesus, spoken before His crucifixion:

> I am the good shepherd; and I know My sheep, and am known by My own. As the Father knows Me, even so I know the Father; and I lay down My life for the sheep ... I lay down My life that I may take it again. No one takes it from Me, but I lay it down of Myself. I have power to lay it down, and I have power to take it again. This command I have received from My Father.
>
> —John 10:14–15, 17–18

Jesus was obedient to His heavenly Father, and the Cross was His supreme act of volunteerism. He *gave* His life voluntarily for our salvation without regard to pain, suffering, mockery, or the disbelief of many who witnessed His death.

Is there any type of service that is beneath you? Is there anything you won't do for Him? God said about King David: "I have found David the son of Jesse, a man after My own heart, who will do all My will" (Acts 13:22). Will God say that about you?

🔖 When have you been forced to serve others against your will? What were the outcomes—in your life and in the lives of others?

But without your consent I wanted to do nothing, that your good deed might not be by compulsion, as it were, but voluntary.

—Philemon 1:14

How is a person's service different if it's done voluntarily rather than by compulsion?

Why would Paul want to ensure that his friend Philemon was serving voluntarily? Why not just force him into it and get the job done?

Principle 2: Without Comparison

A true servant doesn't compare his type of service with that of anyone else. Service is not hierarchical. There is no "top floor, corner office" when it comes to successful service. God looks upon the heart and its motivation in rewarding service, not upon results or achievements.

As we presented in the last lesson, every person is capable and every person is qualified for some type of service. Many people say about service, "I would do more for God if I only had ...." These are only a few of the excuses given in the "if I only had ..." category:

- different job and income.

- different circumstances and time availability.

- different opportunities.

- different family background and status.

Everything that you have is a gift from God, and what you have been given is adequate for the tasks to which He calls you. Rather than focus on what you lack, take a look at what you *have*. Not only do you have adequate talents and gifts with which to serve, but God has given you a place and a people to serve. God has given you your family, your place of employment, your friends, your church, and your neighborhood as opportunities to serve. There are needs all around you. Target *one* of them and get started.

Once you begin to serve, don't criticize those who fail to serve. Jesus did not wash the feet of His disciples and then say to them, "Now you wash My feet." Service must be without criticism and without comparison. Don't criticize your fellow servants. Encourage them and build them up. The person who gives encouragement will also receive encouragement. Offer suggestions when you think that they may be beneficial to the group as a whole, but don't criticize what a person has done in the past or what he is attempting to do. You never know the full story. Only God knows the full extent of that person's effort and the motivation that is behind it.

> For we dare not class ourselves or compare ourselves with those who commend themselves. But they, measuring themselves by themselves, and comparing themselves among themselves, are not wise.
>
> —2 Corinthians 10:12

≈ Put this rather complicated verse into your own words. What exactly is Paul saying?

≈ Why is a person "not wise" if he compares himself with those around him?

⚬◈⚬

Principle 3: No Exclusions

If a person volunteers to join you in your service to others, allow him the privilege of doing so. Nobody is ever too young or too old to serve. In fact, there's no retirement program for Christian service. Following the Lord's example, we are to serve the Lord and to serve others every day of our lives. Jesus called His disciples "little children" during the Last Supper and said to them, "A new commandment I give to you, that you love one another; as I have loved you, that you also love one another. By this all will know that you are My disciples, if you have love for one another" (John 13:34–35). Love knows no age limitations. Even a young child is capable of expressing love and care to others.

Just as you exclude no person from an opportunity to serve, you must also not exclude anyone from receiving service. Consider all whom the Lord Jesus touched with His hands. They included a leper, a child, and a blind man. He used His hands to wash the feet of His disciples. Eventually, He spread His hands out on a cross and died for the sins of all mankind. He certainly expects you to extend your hands to those in need regardless of their race, color, culture, or type of need.

⚬ When have you been excluded from receiving or giving service? How did you feel?

Therefore, from now on, we regard no one according to the flesh.

—2 Corinthians 5:16

*. What does it mean to "regard someone according to the flesh"?

*. When have you treated someone differently because of some "fleshly element"?

Principle 4: Commitment

Regardless of the degree of commitment to service that you may have made in the past, you can make a new start today. Ask God to forgive you for wasted opportunities to serve. Make a commitment to yourself to discover your talents and abilities that might be used in service. Then make a commitment to get involved in the lives of others to help and provide as you are able. A real commitment is one that is acted upon, not merely one that is talked about.

Commitment is required if you are to endure in your service through tough times and persecution. Paul wrote to the Corinthians:

> If anyone builds on this foundation with gold, silver, precious stones, wood, hay, straw, each one's work will become clear; for the Day will declare it, because it will be revealed by fire; and the fire will test each one's work, of what sort it is. If anyone's work which he has built on it endures, he will receive a reward.

> —1 Cor. 3:12–14

Make certain that what you do with your time, energies, and talents is for the gospel, and your work will be counted as gold, silver, and precious stones. It is what you do for your own self-serving interests and self-gratification that will be revealed as wood, hay, and straw.

Commit your works to the Lord, And your thoughts will be established.

—Proverbs 16:3

Commit your way to the Lord, Trust also in Him, And He shall bring it to pass.

—Psalms 37:5

❧ What is the difference between committing our "works" to the Lord and committing our "ways"? Give practical examples of how the two work together.

❦

Principle 5: The Outcome Is God's

You are not responsible fully for the outcomes of your service. Your responsibility is to serve God and others to the best of your ability, with the full force of your love, energy, and talents. What happens as the result of your service is God's responsibility.

The apostle Paul suffered greatly in giving service to the early church. His ministry was filled with conflict, struggles, and troubles. If you were to evaluate Paul's ministry on the basis of the number of times that he was beaten, imprisoned, ridiculed, and scorned, you would consider his ministry to be a total failure. The value of Paul's ministry, however, was not measured by what he went through, but by what God accomplished through his consistent and persistent teaching of the gospel of Jesus Christ.

It is God who saves souls; we merely do the witnessing. It is God who heals and restores; we merely do the "medicating," the praying, and the exhorting. It is God who delivers; we merely proclaim the power, the blood, and the promises made available to us through the name of Jesus. When we serve, God works. He uses everything that we do for His good purposes and eternal plan.

God calls us to be faithful. Our "success" is up to Him. Ministry is not something that we do *for* God, but something that God does *through* us. He is the One who calls us to service, enables us to serve, and produces His desired result from our service. This week, ask the Lord to show you ways to serve others, then pray that He will take care of the results. The rest is up to Him.

[Jesus said] "The Father who dwells in Me does the works."

—John 14:10

Jesus is both God and man, yet He Himself depended upon the Father to produce results from His service. What does this teach us about our own service?

...Whoever is of a willing heart, let him bring it as an offering to the Lord ... They came, both men and women, as many as had a willing heart.

—Exodus 35:5, 22

᠊᠊ᔕ Why does God want us to have a willing heart before we serve Him?

᠊᠊ᔕ What should a Christian do if he does *not* have a willing heart?

Therefore comfort each other and edify one another ... See that no one renders evil for evil to anyone, but always pursue what is good both for yourselves and for all.

—1 Thessalonians 5:11, 15

᠊᠊ᔕ Why does Paul command us to "pursue what is good"? Why not simply tell us to "do good"?

The Lord ... is longsuffering toward us, not willing that any should perish but that all should come to repentance.

—2 Peter 3:9

In what ways has the Lord been longsuffering to you in the past?

Who might you be able to serve this week that you have never thought of serving in the past?

Today and Tomorrow

TODAY: JESUS TEACHES US THAT WE SHOULD HAVE A WILLING HEART TO SERVE ANYONE THAT GOD SENDS OUR WAY.

TOMORROW: I WILL STRIVE THIS WEEK TO SERVE WILLINGLY, LEAVING THE RESULTS IN GOD'S HANDS.

LESSON 10

The Rewards of Service

---———— ❧ **In This Lesson** ❧ ————

LEARNING: WHAT REWARD CAN I EXPECT FROM GOD?

GROWING: HOW CAN I BECOME WORTHY OF REWARD?

————————— ✿ —————————

God rewards service. Nothing that you will ever do in the name of Jesus for another person will go unrewarded by God.

As we stated in Lesson 1, we must be very careful that we *not* count our salvation as one of God's rewards for service. Salvation of one's soul is *not* a reward for our good deeds or our service. Salvation is a free gift from God, motivated solely by His love for us. It is a "grace gift" that we cannot earn and that is never linked to our personal merit (Eph. 2:8–9). What *is* linked to our service is the rewards that the Lord has for us, both in this life and in eternity. Hebrews 6:10 tells us:

> For God is not unjust to forget your work and labor of love which you have shown toward His name, in that you have ministered to the saints, and do minister.

We should never be motivated in our service by the potential for a reward; our motivation should be thanksgiving and love for God and obedience to His command to love our fellow man. But as we serve, we can be assured that God always takes note of our service and that He will reward it.

Our Reward Is from God

When we serve others, we truly are serving the Lord. No matter whom we serve, God says that He is the beneficiary. Ephesians 6:6–8 reminds us that we are "bondservants of Christ, doing the will of God from the heart, with goodwill doing service, as to the Lord, and not to men, knowing that whatever good anyone does, he will receive the same from the Lord, whether he is a slave or free."

It is Christ that we serve, and it is from Christ that we can expect our reward. He is our Master, we are His bondservants. I learned this lesson early in my life as a young teenager delivering newspapers. Very few of the people to whom I delivered newspapers saw me. They simply counted on their newspapers being there when they awoke. It wasn't easy to get up early and do that job—I don't know a teenage boy who wouldn't rather sleep than bundle newspapers and then walk or bicycle a newspaper route. I did my job as unto the Lord, as if I were delivering *His* newspaper each morning.

It was while I was selling newspapers on a street corner that I met a man who was instrumental in my going to college to become a pastor. Was that an accident? I don't believe it was. I believe that God was rewarding those many hours of faithful service. That man was God's *instrument*, but it was from God that I received my reward. It is to our great advantage that our rewards come from God for two main reasons:

1. God alone knows precisely what we need and when we need it. He sees and anticipates our needs long in advance of our feeling or recognizing a need in our own lives, and He provides what is best for us.

2. God alone can give rewards that are eternal. What man can give to us is temporal. Material rewards rust, rot, and wither. Recognition and applause are fleeting. God, in contrast, gives us a deep and abiding fulfillment on this earth, as well as rewards that extend into eternity.

> And whatever you do, do it heartily, as to the Lord and not to men, knowing that from the Lord you will receive the reward of the inheritance; for you serve the Lord Christ.
>
> —Colossians 3:23-24

In practical terms, how do we do things "as to the Lord" rather than "as to men"?

⌘

Rewards Come in Degrees

Not all rewards are alike. God rewards all service, but He does not give out equal rewards for all service. We need to be very clear on this point: A job may be great or small from our perspective, but the act of service is what God sees and rewards. Service is service. God does not give differing rewards because one type of service is of greater or lesser importance than another. Rather, He gives differing rewards on the basis of *our heart motivation and our faithfulness in performing the service.*

Jesus told His disciples a parable about servants who had received different amounts of money—or "talents." The Lord will say to the servants who used their talents to the fullest, "Well done, good and faithful servant; you were faithful over a few things, I will make you ruler over many things. Enter into the joy of your lord" (Matt. 25:21; also v. 23). The servants in this parable were not rewarded on the basis of the amount of money that they were given—in one case five talents; in the other, two. They were not rewarded according to *how* they invested their talents; in fact, Jesus didn't even mention how they used their talents in order to double them. They were rewarded because they were "good and faithful" servants—they performed their service as well as they knew how, and they were faithful and persevering.

Jesus also distinguished between rewards and *great* rewards (Matt. 5:11–12). Those who persevere in their service for the Lord in spite of persecution will receive a *great* reward. Peter asked Jesus what reward he and the other disciples might expect from their faithfulness in serving Him, and Jesus replied (Matt. 19:29):

> Everyone who has left houses or brothers or sisters or father or mother or wife or children or lands, for My name's sake, shall receive a hundredfold, and inherit eternal life.

Mark records Jesus' words here, adding that the faithful would receive a hundredfold *with persecutions* (Mark 10:29–30). The more you are rewarded by God, of course, the more Satan will be upset about your rewards. The enemy of your soul has absolutely no interest in seeing you blessed or honored by God; he detests your prosperity in any form. He will persecute you all the more as you receive greater and greater rewards from the Lord. The good news, however, is that the more you are persecuted for your witness about Jesus Christ, the more your reward grows! The devil's persecutions can never out distance or overwhelm God's rewards on your life. What we can be assured of is that the reward will always be greater than what we give. God multiplies our giving, no matter what form it takes.

Jesus gave another parable about the multiplying of good seed in good soil. This passage relates primarily to the teaching of God's Word, but on a broader level it also includes the unwritten word of our deeds. As Paul wrote, we are "living letters" about the gospel. What we do for others in the form of service is also a means of sowing God's word of love, mercy, and grace into the lives of others. Read Mark 4:3–8 now.

When you give service to others, you are a sower of God's love and of the gospel of Jesus Christ. Be encouraged in your service. At times you may see little or no progress in the lives of those you serve. You may feel as if all the good you are doing evaporates into thin air or is negated. God says that at least *some* of your effort will succeed mightily. God is the One who grows your harvest. Keep on sowing!

> Blessed are you when they revile and persecute you, and say all kinds of evil against you falsely for My sake. Rejoice and be exceedingly glad, for great is your reward in heaven, for so they persecuted the prophets who were before you.
>
> —Matthew 5:11-12

⋞ Notice that the Lord adds the word "falsely" in this verse. Why is that distinction important?

⋞ In practical terms, how does a person rejoice when he is suffering persecution?

Different Types of Rewards

∽ Tangible Rewards ∽

Rewards come in different packages. Some are tangible and material. Luke 6:38 speaks of these types of rewards that God gives us during this life:

> Give, and it will be given to you: good measure, pressed down, shaken together, and running over will be put into your bosom. For with the same measure that you use, it will be measured back to you.

Not all rewards given from man are bad; many gifts that God desires to give to us are the gifts that other people will give to us. If someone attempts to reward you for service that you have rendered, and the gift is moral and legal, the only remaining question to ask is: "How can I use this gift to benefit God's kingdom and bring glory to God?"

We are responsible to God to give an accounting for our stewardship, which is how we use what we have been given by God and others. Paul wrote to the Romans: "So then each of us shall give account of himself to God. Therefore let us not judge one another anymore, but rather resolve this, not to put a stumbling block or a cause to fall in our brother's way" (Rom. 14:12–13). To the Corinthians, Paul wrote: "For we must all appear before the judgment seat of Christ, that each one may receive the things done in the body, according to what he has done, whether good or bad" (2 Cor. 5:10).

A person who gives you a good reward is an agent of God's blessing. That person is God's *ways and means* of providing for you. Thank the person, but above all, thank God for the good reward that He has given to you.

❦ Intangible Rewards ❦

Men are also agents of intangible rewards: praise, admiration, recognition, acknowledgment, and appreciation. It is not wrong to receive a sincere thank-you or public acknowledgment from other people. What is wrong before God is when we serve God and others out of a desire to receive accolades from our fellow man. Jesus was very clear on this point, chiding the Pharisees for making a public display of their fasting, praying, and giving in order that they might appear to be righteous before men. Jesus said to them, "You have your reward." The Pharisees received the praise of others, but that was *all* they would receive. God was not in that reward.

❦ Eternal Rewards ❦

Still other rewards are eternal and will not be received until after we are in heaven. Jesus gave this teaching Luke 14:12–14; take a moment to read it now.

Some rewards will not be given to us until we are resurrected. The Bible refers to at least four types of crowns that will be given to us for our service:

Crown:	Those who will receive it:
Imperishable crown	Those whose hearts' desires have been rooted in obedience (1 Cor. 9:25)
Crown of life	Those who endure temptations, troubles, trials, and heartaches for Christ's sake (James 1:12)

Crown of righteousness	Those who pour out their lives in service of the gospel (2 Tim. 4:8)
Crown of glory that does not fade away	Those who "feed the flock" (1 Peter 5:4)

None of us can truly grasp the glories of heaven. Nor can we begin to imagine or understand all of the blessings that God may have for us in eternity. The rewards that the Lord has for us are immeasurable. None of us can possibly know all of the people that our lives have touched. Service to others has a "ripple" effect that goes beyond our ability to comprehend it. Each time I pick up an inspirational book, I am aware that the author has blessed my life and served me. God will judge and reward each of us for the service that we have given, much of which may occur after we have died.

∞ Conditional Rewards ∞

Some of the rewards that we receive from God are conditional. They are directly related to our obedience. Many of God's commandments are directly related to how we are to serve others; in the Old Testament, these commandments often relate to widows, orphans, and strangers. Other commandments are related to how we serve God through our giving, our sacrifices, and the things that we do for our fellow believers. When we keep God's commandments to serve, we are rewarded. But when we disobey His statutes, we suffer loss.

"I will ... open for you the windows of heaven And pour out for you such blessing That there will not be room enough to receive it."

—Malachi 3:10

 Picture this verse literally happening in your mind. What is implied by the imagery used, such as "open the windows of heaven" and "pour out"?

 ⌘

All in God's Perfect Timing

God chooses the reward that we will receive, and He also chooses *when* we will receive them. As we just discussed, some rewards are immediate, some are in the future of our earthly lives, and still others are granted in eternity. God has just the right time for every reward so that it has maximum effectiveness and benefit in a person's life, and also in the life of the larger body of Christ.

Any farmer will tell you that crops have different growing seasons. A fruit tree sapling may not produce a full harvest for several years. Garden vegetables, by comparison, produce a harvest in a matter of weeks. Trees that are farmed for lumber may take decades to harvest. Our role is not to *force* a reward or to insist that God give us a reward out of season. The younger son in the parable of the Prodigal Son demanded his inheritance out of season and ended up squandering it all (Luke 15:11–24). We are to trust God with patience (Ps. 37). A harvest *will* come, but it will be in God's perfect timing.

This week, ask the Lord to help you trust Him for your rewards. Learning to trust patiently is a great reward in its own right.

And let us not grow weary while doing good, for in due season we shall reap if we do not lose heart. Therefore, as we have opportunity, let us do good to all, especially to those who are of the household of faith.

—Galatians 6:9-10

What conditions must we meet if we are to "reap" a good harvest?

What does it mean to "lose heart" in our service? How can we guard against it?

Do not lay up for yourselves treasures on earth, where moth and rust destroy and where thieves break in and steal; but lay up for yourselves treasures in heaven, where neither moth nor rust destroys and where thieves do not break in and steal.

—Matthew 6:19–20

ᐓ Give some examples of the rewards that most people strive for in the world today. What will become of each of those rewards in 100 years?

ᐓ What are the "treasures in heaven" that the Lord promises us? How do we "lay up" those treasures?

> If then you were raised with Christ, seek those things which are above, where Christ is, sitting at the right hand of God. Set your mind on things above, not on things on the earth.
>
> —Colossians 3:1–2

ᐓ What are the "things above" which we should be seeking? How do we attain those things?

🙢 In practical terms, what does it mean to "set your mind on things above"? How does this compare with setting our minds on "things on the earth"?

Take heed what you hear. With the same measure you use, it will be measured to you; and to you who hear, more will be given. For whoever has, to him more will be given; but whoever does not have, even what he has will be taken away from him.

—Mark 4:24-25

🙢 Jesus is speaking above of hearing the Word of God. Why would He warn us, then, to be careful of what we hear?

🙢 What does it mean that "whoever has" will get more, while "whoever does not have" will lose what little he has?

Do not fear any of those things which you are about to suffer. Indeed, the devil is about to throw some of you into prison, that you may be tested .... Be faithful until death, and I will give you the crown of life.

—Revelation 2:10

In what way would being thrown into prison for serving God be a test? Who is the "test-giver"? What does the test show?

What is "the crown of life"? What is required to receive it?

Today and Tomorrow

TODAY: JESUS ASSURES US THAT WE CAN TRUST GOD TO REWARD OUR SERVICE—BOTH NOW AND LATER.

TOMORROW: THIS WEEK, I WILL ASK THE LORD TO HELP ME TRUST HIM IN ALL THINGS, INCLUDING MY FUTURE REWARD.